Tom Osborne's character, consistency and integrity have always caused me to hold him in high esteem. He recruited me out of high school, and though I did not attend the University of Nebraska, I rooted for them from a distance solely on the basis of the respect I had for their leader. Not only did his players benefit from his example, but I did as well.

Pastor Napoleon Kaufman
Former NFL Running Back
Senior Pastor, The Well Christian Community Church

Victory without honor is an unseasoned dish. It might fill you up, but it won't taste good. I have long admired how Tom Osborne has stood tall in so many arenas, winning with integrity, a humble spirit and honor.

Joe Paterno
Head Football Coach, Pennsylvania State University

Coach Osborne has been one of the most profound role models in my personal and professional life. He is the man we all would hope to be, the coach that we aspire to be, and the selfless leader that has made our nation so great. Our coaches and players will gain a great deal from this terrific book!

Jim Tressel
Head Football Coach, Ohio State University

TOM OSBORNE

DISCOVER A LIFETIME
OF LESSONS LEARNED
ON AND OFF THE FIELD

SECRETS TO

BECOMING

A LEADER

Regal

From Gospel Light
Ventura, California, U.S.A.

Published by Regal
From Gospel Light
Ventura, California, U.S.A.
www.regalbooks.com
Printed in the U.S.A.

This book is excerpted from *Beyond the Final Score*
by Tom Osborne.

Library of Congress Cataloging-in-Publication Data
Osborne, Tom, 1937-
Secrets to becoming a leader : discover a lifetime of
lessons learned on and off the field / Tom Osborne.
p. cm.
ISBN 978-0-8307-5524-0 (trade paper)
1. Christian leadership. 2. Osborne, Tom, 1937- I. Title.
BV652.1.O72 2010
253—dc22
2010016012

Rights for publishing this book outside the U.S.A. or in
non-English languages are administered by Gospel Light
Worldwide, an international not-for-profit ministry.
For additional information, please visit www.glww.org,
email info@glww.org, or write to Gospel Light Worldwide,
1957 Eastman Avenue, Ventura, CA 93003, U.S.A.

To order copies of this book and other Regal products in
bulk quantities, please contact us at 1-800-446-7735.

CONTENTS

INTRODUCTION

As each of us takes our journey through life, we move in and out of various roles. Some of these are common to most people: child, student, neighbor, spouse, parent, coworker, and friend. As teens and then as adults, we take on more specific roles: musician, stockbroker, rancher, chef, counselor, nurse, and so on. I have been blessed to take on a wide variety of roles in my lifetime. I have been a professional athlete, a coach, a congressman, a teacher and an administrator. I have been a leader in various capacities, a public figure, a father and a husband—and a fisherman.

It is my hope that, through it all, I have been able to serve.

For me, leadership begins with being a servant. It is not about accolades, power or prestige. It's about serving over selfishness. This may sound like very idealistic thinking, as we live in a very "me first" society. Servanthood is often the last thing people think about. But I am firmly convinced that the key to unlocking the secrets of great leadership begins with the art of service. All the principles I outline in this book focus around this truth.

Great leadership doesn't happen overnight. It is a process cultivated over time. I think it's important to note that I never consciously said, "I want to be a leader." Generally speaking, I've sought more responsibility in every role I found myself in. As an assistant coach, I wanted to have the responsibility of being a head coach. When I retired from coaching, I thought I could still do something of use and considered going to Washington. I always wanted to be in a position to make my time and efforts count the most, to serve others in some way and ultimately make a positive difference in society.

My life is about developing and using whatever abilities I have to the fullest. I have always wanted to fulfill the opportunities I was given; I didn't want to waste them. I certainly didn't want to look back at the end of my life with regrets concerning things I could have done or should have done.

The secrets of great leadership begin with wanting to take responsibility and to impact those around you, to live your life in service to others. It is my hope that, as I share with you many of the lessons I have learned in my leadership roles, you will be inspired to create a foundation for the leadership role you will play in the future or to enhance the quality of how you lead others today. Each of us is given many opportunities to lead, and you are no exception. I hope that this book will cause you to look at leadership from what may be a different perspective, which will benefit those around you.

1

LEADERSHIP STYLES

There are effective leaders and there are ineffective leaders—and I've been both at one time and another. I think that one thing I've had going for me is that I have always tried to learn from my mistakes. I believe that this is an essential quality for anyone who desires to grow into effective leadership.

I have been in various leadership positions for many years, and that means I've had plenty of chances to make mistakes and learn from them. I have also had a lot of time to observe both effective and ineffective leaders at work and to learn from their mistakes and successes. One thing I have noticed: worldview and effective leadership are often linked. In the leadership courses I've taught over the years, I have tried to help my students make this connection because I think it is so important.

How a person leads is greatly influenced by his or her understanding of the world. Leaders are called on each day to make decisions that affect the lives of many people, and those decisions must be based on a foundation more solid than feelings, opinion polls or personal preferences. This is why I believe that worldviews are inextricably tied to leadership.

When I was coaching, we began each season by gathering our coaching staff to write our coaching philosophy for that season. What principles would we adhere to in dealing with players, staff members and each other? What values would we model to our athletes? We also collectively wrote our offensive and defensive philosophies. Were we an attacking or a reading defense? Offensively, did we emphasize the run or the pass?

A mental picture of what our program should look like preceded playing the games. In a similar way, a worldview precedes how we live our lives. As a Christian, I understand there are principles we are meant to live by, aligned with good instead of evil, and that realization is what transforms us from the inside out. If you trust a moral authority that transcends your own feelings, opinions and experiences, you will usually make decisions based on that worldview and live life according to those principles.

The same is true as it concerns leadership in business, politics, community and family. As we explore the characteristics of several different kinds of leaders, keep this connection between worldview and leadership in mind.

Laissez-Faire Leaders

I believe there are three basic approaches to leadership. The first is a "laissez-faire" (hands-off) approach, which is, in a sense, an absence of leadership. You might say, "Well, that really isn't a type of leadership," but I would answer that there are a lot of people who have the title of "leader" but who really avoid leading. When they are pressed into making a decision, they often boycott their own leadership.

I saw this in politics quite often. For example, a governor who has pledged not to raise taxes may choose to defer to the state legislature when a severe economic crisis reduces tax revenues to the point that there is no option left but to raise taxes. The State Patrol, Medicaid recipients, schools, roads and other entities require state money and can't endure cuts beyond a certain point, so the governor forces the legislature to find ways to keep the state running, which means tax increases. The governor then vetoes these tax increases and keeps his pledge to his constituents, knowing full well that the legislature will have to override the veto and take the political hit. The point is, however, that someone has to decide which taxes to raise and by how much, how the revenues will be allocated, and which programs will be cut or streamlined. Laissez-faire leadership lets someone else make the tough decisions.

Laissez-faire political leaders are concerned about protecting their image at all costs, so you can never be sure where they stand on an issue. They take a poll, find out what people want to hear, and then make decisions based on what will get votes or approval ratings. It's a popularity contest in which they seize on those things that seem to resonate with people—their hot buttons. They refuse to take a position on the tough issues, or they only give a vague response when asked to comment on a particular concern, which allows them to straddle the fence.

Many laissez-faire leaders avoid responsibility by appointing a committee. I once knew a football coach who hired offensive and defensive coordinators who made all the calls during a game. The head coach would never make a decision himself but would criticize the coordinators unmercifully if their calls didn't work. As a result, the coordinators were unwilling to take necessary risks and limited themselves to "safe" calls that were less likely to draw fire from the head coach.

You can't lead that way. As a leader, you have to take responsibility for decisions you make—whether they work out or not. I saw this behavior exemplified in University of Nebraska head coach Bo Pelini after the painful loss we had against Missouri in 2008. Some coaches would have come into the locker room and screamed or cursed at the players. Bo came in and said, "I gave you a game plan that was too complicated for you to execute. That's my fault." He offered encouragement to his players and shouldered the blame when he later met with the press. This gesture solidified his assistant coaches and his players. They knew that they would not be sacrificed to appease the fans.

In business, I see leaders who are reluctant to tackle the tough issues. If there's something difficult or controversial, they make excuses about needing more information before they decide the correct course to take. They may put together a task force and say, "Let's let this team study these things and come back with a recommendation. Then we'll think about taking action based on what they say." They rarely say, "I believe that this is where the company needs to go, and we're going to begin making the tough decisions that are necessary to get us to that place." They simply put off making decisions, with the result that those who are under them are often left with no direction. Laissez-faire type leadership is much more prevalent than people think.

Transactional Leaders

The second approach to leadership is often referred to as transactional leadership. This is the most common leadership style, in which the leader says, "If you do this for me, I'll do that for you. If you work overtime, you'll get paid extra. If you do a good job on this report, I'll give you more responsibility. If you do what I tell you to do and you're always on time and you work hard, I'll give you a raise." It's this for that, and it's traditionally how most people and companies conduct business. Transactional leaders reward good performance and punish bad performance; they focus on external outcomes such as turning a profit, passing grades or winning games.

Research indicates that, generally speaking, a system of reward works better than one that threatens punishment, but in transactional leadership both elements are present: "If you're late again, we're going to dock your pay. If you don't play well this week, you're going to go to the second team. If you don't get your expense report in by a certain date, your budget will be cut." If things get too negative, morale suffers.

Further, this model of leadership sometimes results in something I call "passive punishment." An example would be an employee thinking that he is doing a great job, when all of a sudden he gets a negative performance review. Nobody told him that there was a problem or that he needed to do anything differently, and now it's too late—it's in his file. Or maybe that woman in the cube across the hall from you gets fired. Nobody ever had a clue that anything was wrong; one day she's just gone, and everyone starts looking over their shoulder, wondering if they're next. This is why, when I was a coach, we graded our players on every play and reviewed game films and their grades before we announced any changes on the depth chart. We tried to keep them informed about how they were doing every step of the way.

A passive-punishment environment can be damaging to an organization. It fosters a poisonous culture that pits people against each other and engenders a lack of trust in leadership. Passive transactional leadership creates a culture of fear. At times, people lose their jobs, are demoted or must take a pay cut. If leaders are continually providing feedback on areas that need improvement or provide information regularly on market conditions that may result in layoffs or pay cuts, an organization can still function effectively. Negative episodes with no feedback or warning are destructive in any organization.

One might get the impression that every leader neatly falls exclusively into one category or another. It has been my observation, however, that reality often doesn't match theory. The most decisive, hard-driving transactional leader may occasionally duck a hard decision by appointing a committee, thereby showing a laissez-faire streak. Someone who is mostly a servant leader (I'll explore that in detail in the next chapter) occasionally has to administer reward and punishment. The person who ordinarily ducks decision-making like the plague may suddenly and decisively administer reward

and punishment. Most leaders, most of the
time, however, exhibit one style over another.

There Is a Better Way

When I first took over as head coach in 1973, it
wasn't all a bed of roses, as I was coaching players who had been recruited by Bob Devaney and
who had great loyalty and affection toward him.
I was also working with coaches who had been
hired by Bob, and most of them had been with
him at the University of Wyoming. Some had
even been with him when he was a high school
coach in Michigan. As a result, I was the new guy
on the block, and even though I had been an assistant at Nebraska, I'm sure I was seen as someone who had not necessarily earned his spurs.

I probably wasn't as effective in regard to
leadership during my first few years as head
coach. In *Heart of a Husker*, edited by Mike Bab-
cock, one player who was a senior my first year
as head coach in 1973 wrote this: "It didn't feel
the same with Coach Osborne as it did with
Coach Devaney. And maybe, again, that was obviously a difference in personalities. It just
was . . . Devaney was just different. He was more
of a gambler, put it out on the line, and Tom was
an *X*s-and-Os type of guy."

Over time, however, I did develop a style of
leadership that made sense to me and was em-
braced by my players. This leadership style is

most often referred to as "transformational" leadership. A transformational leader is one who is a role model, is visionary, inspires, listens empathetically, and has values workers want to emulate. Instead of telling a player, employee, or coworker how stupid they are after they make a mistake, tell them you know they can do better and make sure they know how to perform correctly. You will change behavior much faster if you are rewarding and praising the behavior you desire than if you are constantly criticizing and berating. I was far from perfect as a transformational leader, but it made sense to me to lead in this way. I got better at it over time.

People who are guided by servant leadership feel valued, trusted and empowered and respond with a high level of performance. I remember a particular instance when I was having conversations with Creighton basketball coach Dana Altman. The coach was having a hard time getting through to a player from a rough background and he asked me to sit down with this troubled young man. I didn't say much to him; I mostly listened. This young man was very close to his grandmother. Apparently she was ill and he was really worried about her, and that was affecting his life in school and on the court. Sitting down with the player and hearing where he was coming from was fundamental in improving his performance. A big thing in leading others transformationally is listening to what they have to say. When people feel understood and appreciated, they often are energized and freed up to perform at higher levels.

Some may believe this leadership style makes a leader appear soft or too nice, but it is my experience in using this approach with my players, congressional staff and athletic department, that it led them to play harder, work harder and focus on excellence.

2

TRANSFORMATIONAL LEADERSHIP

Transformational, or what some people call servant, leadership is effective but also complex and, at times, difficult. All the principles I discuss in this book relate directly to transformational leadership—whether empowering others, bringing unity, or making a difference.

Leading in this way often springs from a Christian worldview. Jesus said that whoever wants to become great must become a servant of all (see Mark 10:43). Of course, servant leaders may come from other faiths and from other worldviews. Whatever their background, however, transformational leaders are not all that common.

Research shows that transformational leaders are often more effective, but that it is more demanding to be an effective transformational leader. They hope and plan for good external outcomes, but their effectiveness relies on adherence to principles and an ability to cultivate strong relationships, cohesiveness and a sense of common purpose rather than on extrinsic goals and rewards.

Transformational business leaders focus on releasing creativity and innovation (which often leads to an increase in profits). Transformational teachers and mentors focus on helping students apply new knowledge to their lives (which often leads to excellent grades). Transformational coaches focus on building teams whose members trust each other and work together seamlessly (which often leads to a better win-loss record). But profits, good grades and wins are not the focus; they are a byproduct.

Early in my career, I was more of a transactional leader. I felt pressure to carry on the legacy begun by Bob Devaney, and focused my energies on the bottom line: winning football games.

As time went on, however, and as I thought and read more about being a good leader, I realized that I had a choice. (John Wooden's books, and later Stephen Covey's work, helped to crystallize this choice in my mind.) I could continue serving the outcomes I desired, or I could choose to serve the people I was called to lead. Servant leadership is difficult because the leader is required to exemplify characteristics that are often rare:

1. The leader is willing to sacrifice self-interest for the good of the group.
2. The leader is willing to listen empathetically to understand followers.

3. The leader is a role model—exemplifies qualities that followers admire.
4. The leader is able to communicate and inspire others toward a shared vision.
5. The leader's actions are rooted in principles and values rather than in external rewards.
6. The leader encourages growth and increased responsibility in followers.
7. The leader is dedicated to having his or her organization serve others and be a constructive force in society.
8. The leader has exceptional awareness and vision—he or she can anticipate future trends and events.

Throughout most of my coaching career, I was not aware of transformational leadership. I had never even heard the term. However, intuitively, I was drawn to the fundamental principles of this leadership style.

Servant-Coach

It didn't happen all at once, but I began to shift my focus away from the outcomes I wanted and toward the people around me. I began to listen to and value their thoughts and opinions more. I tried to inspire and motivate rather than reward and punish. As a football coach, I spent more time with players in the weight room, at meals and after practice, and as I did I began to see them as valuable for who they were instead of for what they could do.

As time went by, at the start of each new season, I gathered the whole team and staff together and briefly talked about where I was coming from philosophically and spiritually. There were no high-pressure tactics to get everyone to agree with me or to make some kind of spiritual commitment; I just wanted everyone to know that my beliefs were the driving force behind my leadership and decision-making. Since I would be making decisions that would affect their lives, I thought it was appropriate for me to let them know the philosophical genesis of most of those decisions. I'm sure that some players appreciated my openness, while others probably wondered what this had to do with football. However, I believed that the way people were treated had a lot to do with team chemistry, and that chemistry had a lot to do with football.

My last 10 years or so of coaching, I began to focus on hiring and mentoring coaches who also had a transformational approach to leadership. It was important to me that they had a strong spiritual center out of which came their ideas about how to treat players and create teams. I also wanted them to be positive role models for the young men in the program, people to look up to and want to emulate. Some days we were better role models than others, but we always cared about the players, regardless of their level of contribution on the field.

Each of us is called on to play various roles throughout our lives. It is my belief that in every phase of life and in every professional and relational role we play, we should choose servanthood over selfishness. Of course, this is very idealistic thinking, as we live in a very "me first" society and servanthood is often the last thing people think about. As I reflect back over my life, I can see many times when I have been selfish and have not been a servant; however, I hope that the general thrust of my leadership style during the last 40-plus years has moved more in the direction of servanthood and less toward self-serving.

When I first started coaching, there was no such thing as a "shoe contract," a phrase that is as common now in college sports as "sponsored by Gatorade®." When Nebraska was first approached by one of the leading shoe manufacturers about setting up a sponsorship for which they would furnish shoes to all of our players, one of the offers on the table made me very uncomfortable: The company would pay me if the athletes wore that company's brand of shoe.

That didn't seem right to me—and I wasn't the only coach who thought so. Why should coaches get paid for what our players wear on their feet? Several head coaches, all around the same time, decided that such a thing was not in the best interests of our players. Bo Schembechler at Michigan refused to take the "shoe money" (as it came to be called), and at Nebraska we used the money to set up a post-graduate scholarship fund for players who decided to pursue further education.

There is a stark contrast between coaches who are in it for themselves and those who serve their players. On the one hand, you see coaches like the young high school coach I met on a recruiting trip years ago. "Man, I just love this job," he told me. "It's just amazing the power that I have over these kids. I can tell 'em to do almost anything and they'll do it." I was appalled. All I could think was, *I'm glad my son is not playing for this guy.*

Coaching, for that young man, was about gratifying his ego by exercising power. For others, it is about financial gain or publicity or status. Yet many people who choose to play the role of coach do so out of a sincere love for players and their sport. They put their players first, never putting someone in the game who is at serious risk for injury or benching a player out of spite. They refuse to cut corners when it comes to recruiting or to bend or break the rules to get an edge over the competition. They honor and respect their opponents in word and in deed, on and off the field.

It's often easy to tell the difference between these two kinds of coaches by looking at their

teams. Players coached by self-seeking leaders
are often not team-oriented and can be disrup-
tive. They often tear others down and lash out
when they are not on the first team, and they
sometimes have behavior problems that are difficult to get under control.

If a coach has enticed a player using unethical recruiting promises, their relationship is out
of balance from the word "go"; a coach who had
offered a player illegal inducements once con-
fided to me, "You know, once you've done that,
your coach-player relationship is forever altered.
He has power over you that he should not have
because he can turn you in or use it against you.
The whole dynamic is undermined, and in the
long run, the team is put at risk."

By contrast, players coached by leaders who
put their players' interests ahead of their own
usually play with heart, drive and determination,
even when they are having a tough season; they
play hard because they know that their coach will
never deliberately sacrifice their welfare for his
own. They speak to and act toward their teammates and opponents alike with respect, and
they understand that their behavior choices will
have an effect on everyone. In short, these players learn under the tutelage of a servant-coach,
and through the ups and downs of the game,
what it means to be a person of strong character.

Having a servant mentality was something I
stressed to the players. Brook Berringer, the

quarterback for the University of Nebraska in the mid-1990s, exemplified this kind of leadership best. Brook came from Goodland, Kansas, a small town in the western part of the state, and before he came to Nebraska, I doubt that he had played in front of a crowd of more than 500 people.

Tommie Frazier, a quarterback from Bradenton, Florida, came to school about the same time. He had played in the Florida state championship game in front of more than 60,000 people. He was all-star material from the get-go, and he started for us as a freshman. He led the team to victory in the first four games of the '94 season, and then was diagnosed with blood clots in his leg and could not play the remainder of the season.

We needed a quarterback to fill the gap, and we turned to Brook. Honestly, we didn't know exactly what to expect—Tommie had been our go-to guy, and much of our offense was structured around his talent. On top of that, the players were united behind Tommie and uncertain about how to move forward without his leadership. We needn't have worried. Brook stepped in and led the team to eight straight wins, and gave the players the confidence they needed to pull together.

Brook did all this with a lung that collapsed twice. His condition was serious enough that we started our number three quarterback, Matt

Turman, against Kansas State in Manhattan, Kansas. Matt performed well, but the game was tight and Brook wanted to play. I asked the doctor if it was possible to play Brook; he said it would be okay as long as he "didn't get hit." Naturally, a player not getting hit in football is hard to guarantee; however, Brook did enter the game in the second half and did a great job of leading us to victory. We won the game 17-6. Our defense was outstanding, and Brook played very well. We continued to win and finished the regular season with a 13-3 win over the University of Oklahoma in Norman.

By the time the bowl game in Miami rolled around, Tommie Frazier had recovered to the point that he was allowed to play. We had a major scrimmage prior to the bowl game and Tommie graded slightly better than Brook, so Tommie started—but Brook came in and threw a touchdown pass during the second quarter. They both played significant roles in the game, and we won 24-17. That win sealed an undefeated season and the National Championship.

Here's where the servant part comes in: At the start of the 1995 season, Nebraska had two great quarterbacks who together had led our team to a national championship the previous year. Who would be the starter and who the backup? We decided that we would grade every snap during our fall camp going into the 1995 season. This included scrimmages and practices. At the end of fall camp, the grades were almost identical; however, Brook Berringer had one interception in our final scrimmage and Tommie had none. So we named Tommie Frazier as our starting quarterback and Brook was once again the backup.

Now, it wouldn't be too hard to find a quarterback of Brook Berringer's caliber who, put in a similar position, would have caused dissention. There were many team members who would have supported him had Brook decided to do so—he had won the players' gratitude and loyalty when he had led them through such a trying time of uncertainty the previous year. And many players would have supported Tommie. Yet Brook chose to sacrifice what some might have seen as his right to raise a fuss in favor of supporting Tommie and the team. He was always encouraging, always positive.

In a 2006 readers' poll on ESPN.com, the 1995 Cornhuskers were voted the best college football team of all time. There is no doubt in my mind that the chemistry, heart and cohesiveness of that team were due in no small part to the servanthood of Brook Berringer. Without his self-sacrifice, the team might easily have disintegrated into factions instead of coming together as the best team that I had the privilege of coaching.

Brook was a man of uncommonly strong faith. He was an excellent role model and did a great deal of community outreach, speaking to school children, visiting hospitals, and reading to kids. He influenced many of Nebraska's players to seek deeper meaning in their lives and I'm confident that, if he had lived, he would have made a similar impact on players in the NFL. An amateur airplane pilot, Brook was flying a small plane when it crashed near Raymond, Nebraska, two days before the NFL draft. He was killed in the crash, along with his friend Tobey Lake, who was also his fiancée's brother. Nearly 50,000 people honored Brook in a ceremony held in Memorial Stadium prior to the 1996 spring football game. That crowd stood as a witness to the great person, football player and servant that Brook was.

When you are in a position to lead others in a transformational way—whether you are serving on a sports team, a PTA committee, a volunteer organization, or a small group at church—you have the opportunity to bring out the best in those you serve and, ultimately, the best in the organization you lead.

Serving in Political Office

When we opened my congressional office, our policy was to answer each and every piece of constituent mail that we received within 14 days. On an average day, we received between 150 and 200 letters, in addition to the 50 or so emails delivered to the inbox. Answering each one in a timely fashion was a time-consuming and never-ending job, but our view was that responding to our constituents' needs and concerns was the whole point of being a congressional representative. It was one of many forms of service.

Serving Nebraska's Third District, however, entailed much more than answering mail. I believed that the best way I could serve the residents of the Third District was to listen to their concerns, ideas and aspirations and then articulate a vision for our future. To be an effective leader, it is important to paint a picture of what can be and take concrete steps to make the possible happen.

One concern I heard again and again from constituents was the loss of young people from our rural district—young adults were heading off to college and not coming back. An entire way of life was beginning to die out as the older generation retired or passed away, and no one was coming to take their places. How could we stem the tide of "brain drain" and keep Nebraska's best and brightest rooted and growing in our communities? Many bright young people from rural areas wanted to stay, but the lack of good jobs drove them away. How about having them create their own job?

We thought that one way would be to educate the younger generation on entrepreneurship. We put together an entrepreneurial handbook that showed young people the nuts and bolts of starting a business. What's your idea? How do you plan on implementing it? How do you write a business plan? How do you obtain a grant or loan? Our vision was to inspire creative and innovative young people to start businesses that would eventually create jobs and prosperity in communities that might have died without them.

A number of communities incorporated entrepreneurial training in their school systems and many used the entrepreneurial handbook as a starting point. The value of this program was that a student learned what it took to start a business that would have a chance of being successful. In the future, they would not shy away from developing a new business that might employ other people in their community if they ran across an idea that could be financially feasible and productive. Many times, people won't try to start a business because they have no idea of how to do it. I know that many small businesses were started throughout the Third District as a result of these entrepreneurial training programs.

I also heard many Third District residents express their dismay at the growing methamphetamine problem in our state. As in many other parts of the country, meth use was beginning to become an epidemic. Somewhere in the neighborhood of 50 percent of children in

Nebraska's foster-care system were there because their parents were meth addicts—these folks had lost their ability to care about anything but the drug, and that included their kids.

There are tremendous social costs to this kind of family breakdown, but there are also financial costs: a dependent meth user costs the U.S. nearly $75,000 per year. Taken together, the annual cost of meth to our society is estimated to be more than $23 billion! By my estimate, Nebraska's share of this cost is $1.5 billion annually. That only represents the financial cost—the human cost is even greater. One of my college classmates lost his bright, college-student daughter when she got confused in a snow storm, couldn't think or communicate effectively and died from exposure because of meth.

How could our congressional office help to tackle this rampant problem? We decided that one way was to pull together an educational DVD to be shown in Nebraska schools that would inform students about the dangers of methamphetamine and alcohol abuse. Our goal was to get the DVD into the hands of every school administrator in the state within one year and to appear at a school assembly in every high school and middle school in the Third District. I am certain that many lives were saved in the process. At nearly every presentation, we had students approach us with stories about what meth and alcohol had done to their families.

Whether our office was tackling meth use, water shortages, brain drain or our bottomless pile of mail, the driving force behind our efforts was to serve the people I was elected to represent. As a matter of fact, we wrote a formal mission statement that stated our purpose was "to serve the people of the Third District of Nebraska." I know that many other politicians view their positions in this way, and I believe these folks are the most effective at their jobs. Our representative democracy can be of the people, by the people and for the people, when the goal is to serve rather than be served. Unfortunately, for many in politics, the mission is to get elected or re-elected rather than serve.

One of the best examples of a servant leader that I saw in Congress was a congressman from North Carolina named Robin Hayes. Robin's family had been in the textile business for many years, and many of Robin's constituents were textile workers. These jobs were leaving North Carolina and going overseas, where labor costs are much cheaper.

One night, we had a long session followed by a vote on the Central America Free Trade Agreement (CAFTA). Robin knew that a vote for that trade agreement would be very unpopular in his district, as many people would perceive it as legislation that would cause more jobs to go overseas. Many labor groups were and are opposed to trade agreements, as they would rather see an isolationist approach in which the U.S. erects trade barriers and keeps foreign products out of the United States. The problem with this approach is that other countries will not buy goods from us in return if we exclude their products from our markets. We have a global economy in which goods and commodities are sold and traded worldwide. A protectionist approach is therefore self-defeating.

Robin knew very well that his vote for CAFTA could cost him his next election, yet he also believed strongly that CAFTA would serve the greater good in the United States and throughout the world by creating more jobs and trade. The leadership was counting on Robin to help pass the bill, and he eventually pushed the green button in favor of the bill. He had tears in his eyes when he did so, because he knew that his political future was very bleak at that point.

Robin did survive one more election—barely—and then lost in the 2008 elections. However, he voted as he did based on principle and what he thought was best for the country rather than getting himself re-elected. I'm not sure how many people in Washington would do what Robin did. There are a few, undoubtedly, but not very many.

Servant-Leader

I'd like to add two additional thoughts here.

The first is to point out what I think is the obvious connection between servanthood and character. Essentially, being a servant demands that one be a person of good character, and vice versa. Honesty, integrity, generosity, a sense of fair play—these are all attributes that we associate with people of good character, and they are remarkably consistent across eras and cultures, as Stephen Covey and others have noted. If anyone wants to be a good leader—that is, if he or she hopes that others will follow him or her—these are essential attributes that must be developed. People may follow a corrupt, charismatic personality or a visionary without substance for a while, but if their leader lacks character, eventually they will find someone else to follow. (There are times, however, as in the case of Adolf Hitler, when it takes a distressingly long time to see what the leader is all about.)

The second point is that a core aspect of being a leader is challenging those who follow us to display good character. Sometimes this aspect of leadership means a willingness to confront followers for bad choices and behaviors. While confrontation makes many people uncomfortable, it is occasionally necessary.

I recruited a young man years ago who was rumored to be a marijuana user in high school. We wanted to offer him a scholarship, but we had a strict no-drugs policy. I decided that the best course of action was to ask him up-front: "We want to recruit players, not problems. Have you used or do you use marijuana?"

The young man said, "No, absolutely not. I would never use drugs." I took him at his word and we moved forward in the process, offering him a scholarship for the following fall.

About three months before players were to report for practice, we sent out a notice that they each had to undergo a physical exam to ensure that they were in good health. We also notified them that they would be drug tested. The players arrived in early August, were given physical exams and were tested for steroids and street drugs. When the young man's results came in, I saw that he had tested positive for marijuana use.

So, I called him in. "Remember what you told me? You said that you had never used marijuana and never would. You weren't honest with me, and by telling a lie, you have broken trust with me. Here's the thing: I still care about you and want to help make you the best player you can be. But from here on out, it's going to be tough. We're going to notify your parents. We're going to send you for a drug evaluation to determine if you need counseling or a drug rehabilitation hospital. We're going to test you weekly from now on. Can you live with that?"

Well, the player wasn't happy about it, but he agreed to my terms and joined the team under the conditions that we had set for him. Unfortunately, over the next six months, he tested positive for drug use two more times. According to our policy, he was dismissed for good.

That young man was a fine football player, and I would have liked to have had him on the team. His suspension was not just a loss for him but also a loss for all of us. However, leading in that situation meant challenging that young man to be a better person—in essence, serving his long-term good by sacrificing the team's short-term gain. About 10 years later, I got a call from the young player. He apologized to me for lying and for his drug use, expressing remorse for his behavior. He was now drug-free after having had a spiritual conversion, and was trying to make things right.

Even though it might entail a short-term loss for the whole group, leaders rarely go wrong when they are determined to serve the character development of their individual followers. Sometimes this service, in the form of a challenge, is rejected at the time only to bear fruit much later. But it is always worth waiting for.

3

EMPOWER

When you are in a position of leadership, you have to lead those who follow you with dignity and respect, giving them the space to carry out what they are responsible to do and encouraging them on their way. It is my experience that this is done by building up others, not tearing them down. This also helps to cultivate an environment of success—where ideas are generated, objectives are carried out, confidence is built, and productivity thrives.

Accentuate the Positive

In the book *How Full Is Your Bucket?* Don Clifton and Tom Rath outline the tragedy that happened with American prisoners during the Korean War. The highest percentage of all recorded prisoner deaths occurred during this war, even though the prisoners were not tortured and were reasonably well fed.

The high death rate resulted primarily from the negative environment in which the POWs lived. They were rewarded if they informed on each other and if they confessed things they had done during their lifetime of which they were ashamed. Any news from home that was negative was quickly brought to them, but anything of a supportive or positive nature was kept from them. The negativism took a toll, and many prisoners lost their will to live and simply succumbed to despair. Thirty-eight percent of these POWs died.

Don Clifton, one of the authors of the book, was an associate of mine in the Department of Educational Psychology at the University of Nebraska. Don formulated a new approach to psychology based on much of the research he had done. At the time I met Don back in the 1960s, psychology focused heavily on the study of animals as they were conditioned to behave in certain ways through reward and punishment. Psychology was also heavily oriented toward deviant behavior and the study of various mental illnesses.

Don reasoned that if we want exceptional behavior, we would benefit from studying those who perform exceptionally well. At one point, he was asked to develop a personality inventory that would help identify the very best insurance salesmen. Don studied the top producers in the insurance industry and tried to identify traits they shared in common. He also looked at those who were not successful in selling insurance and examined what traits they did not have in common with the top producers.

Don then developed a survey composed of questions that successful insurance salesmen tended to answer one way and unsuccessful salesmen tended to answer differently. Using this survey, he was able to assist insurance companies in hiring people who were more likely to succeed. It sounds simple, but hardly anyone was studying top performers and excellence in those days. The emphasis was always on the subpar and the abnormal.

From this research, Don began to formulate a theory that each of us is like a bucket and that each of us has a dipper. We can put positive messages and information into other people's buckets, or we can, through negativism, deplete the reservoir of positive self-image in the bucket of others. Even though this seems rather common sense today, at the time it was almost totally outside the scope of conventional psychology.

Don observed that positive comments and feedback must outnumber negative interchanges in close personal relationships, such as between family members, by a ratio of at least 5 to 1. When the number of positive and negative interchanges began to approach 1 to 1, divorce and dysfunction were likely to follow. In the workplace, he noted that a 3 to 1 positive ratio was indicative of a cohesive, productive workplace; anything less than that percentage resulted in a great deal of negativism and dysfunction.

So, what does all this have to do with the high death rate of Korean War POWs? Well, Don reasoned that if bad news from home, informing on each other and a breakdown in the chain of command could have such terrible outcomes, then maybe the opposite behavior could create positive results. He believed that an environment that recognized and celebrated desired performance—one that emphasized praise rather than condemnation and one in which people worked together in a spirit of support and encouragement—would unleash creativity, energy and productivity.

I came to believe that catching a player doing something right and reinforcing it with praise was much more effective in shaping behavior than catching him doing something wrong and punishing him for it. Many times, people equate coaching with criticizing and punishing, and it is true that much coaching is of this nature. However, I don't believe it is as effective as providing a great deal of positive feedback.

I had lunch a few years ago with the Commandant of the Marine Corps, General Charles Krulak. We were comparing basic training in the Marines with pre-season football training. General Krulak told me that the Corps had changed its approach to its new recruits: In times gone by, the point of basic training was to break down each recruit's will so that he or she would follow orders no matter what. But, he said, the focus now was on building teams.

Why? Because somewhere along the line, the Corps did its research and found that the reason

Marines would go charging up a hill in the face of machine gun fire wasn't because they were trained to follow orders no matter what; the reason was that they cared so much for their fellow Marines, and they didn't want to let them down. In light of this new understanding, the Corps changed its approach to basic training to focus much more on building strong relationships among the Marines and forming cohesive teams.

So that's what they did. The Marine Corps trainers tried to catch trainees doing something right, and they found that rewarding good work got them further much faster than punishing mistakes and humiliating new recruits.

Unfortunately, there are still remnants of the old military basic training approach within coaching circles. Coaches perpetuate this practice because they were coached that way as young athletes and assume that this is the only effective way to coach. I once had a high school coach from Nebraska thank me for showing him and others that there was another way to achieve top performance. This coach won numerous state championships after abandoning some of his "old school" practices.

I tried to approach coaching players in the same way—catch them doing something right—and encouraged my staff to do the same. Instead of tearing a player down for doing something wrong, we emphasized what they were already doing right. "Tackle, you put your head up, locked your arms and drove your feet. That's a great example of what we're looking for." Even when correction was necessary, it was possible to do it in a positive way: "Tackle, I've seen you do it right a thousand times, and I know you can do this. You're doing great with your locked arms and your feet positioned, but you've got to keep your head up."

I made it clear to the coaching staff that there was no place for humiliating or dehumanizing players. On the rare occasion when one of the coaches got caught up in the heat of the moment (usually during a game) and began to berate a player, I'd try to remind him, "Don't just tell him what he did wrong—tell him how to do it right." A player who has made a mistake usually knows that he has made a mistake—he doesn't need someone to tell him, and he certainly doesn't need someone to tell him what a useless player and terrible human being he is. He needs someone to tell him how to fix it, and that's what a coach is for. Our coaches were very positive for the most part. I recall the time Lou Holtz, who was then coaching at Arkansas, visited Nebraska and watched us practice and sat in on our meetings. Before he left he told me that the one thing that most impressed him was how positive our coaches were and how little negativism or humiliation he observed. It was nice to have a coach of Lou's experience and stature pick up on that aspect of our program.

One of the most effective and cheapest ways an organization can boost productivity and reduce conflict and even illness is to systematically reward and praise exceptional effort and performance. According to the Department of Labor, the main reason people leave their jobs is because they don't feel appreciated.

Focusing on the positive and trying to catch players doing something right did not mean that players never suffered consequences for poor behavior. But our policy was to punish poor behavior, not mistakes. If it was clear that a player was making a habit of giving less than full effort or was deliberately ignoring instructions, we put him on the bench. If he didn't go to class, we put him on the bench. But when we did so, we invested time and energy into finding out what was beneath the player's behavior. Was there something going on at home? Was he worried about his classes? Did he have a conflict with someone on the team? Sure, there were a handful of players over the years who were downright lazy or who had bad attitudes—but in my experience, the vast majority of people want to do the right thing and just need help doing it.

In the end, this approach to leadership and team building is related to my faith. I believe that each and every person should be treated with the dignity and respect that they deserve and that they should know they are valued and appreciated.

Empowering My Staff

When those you lead—people on your particular staff, committee, team, or even those in your family—experience the kind of transformational leadership that is encouraging and uplifting, they feel empowered and confident to perform at a high capacity. As a congressman, it was important to me that my staff felt empowered to carry out their roles. I had to make clear that I trusted them to support me and believed that they were more than capable of executing their tasks well.

When I first arrived in Washington, we drew numbers to determine which vacant office we could choose. My number was 39 out of 39 (there were technically 41 freshman, but the other two had special arrangements for their offices), so theoretically it was the worst office in the House of Representatives. We were located on the fifth floor of the Cannon Building, which could not be reached by all the elevators. Actually, the Cannon Building wasn't all that bad; John Kennedy once had an office there. The main negative about my particular office suite, Cannon 507, was that it was about one-half mile from the House floor. I walked three to four miles a day just voting.

I didn't do my job alone. We had seven or eight staff members in Nebraska and about the same number on Capitol Hill, and in the early days it seemed they were reluctant to act on

their own. Every letter ready to be sent, every
meeting that needed someone to attend—no
one felt they could go ahead and do what
needed to be done without clearing it through
the chief of staff or me.

It was obvious that, in order to serve 600,000
constituents, we could not have that kind of
bottleneck. So I set out a general guideline:
serve the people. If serving the people means
going to a meeting or writing a letter or giving
a speech, don't call me or the chief of staff to
get approval. Do it. You were hired because
you're capable and because we trust you to
make judgments about how things need to get
done. If someone made a mistake, I would take
the heat, not that person.

Every letter was proofread before it went out
to make sure there were no glaring mistakes,
but I managed my congressional staff just as I
have managed other people over the years:
Make the mission clear and trust people to accomplish it. I was fortunate to have an excellent
staff of 16 people. Each person had specific areas of responsibility, and as time went on, we
began to function effectively as a team.

A Focus on Values

When I was head coach, I tried not to micromanage my assistants. If an offensive coach had
drills that he preferred to run, great—attending

to that kind of detail was his job, and he could do so with a certain level of autonomy. My job was to attend to the larger principles that would create a healthy environment and winning football team.

I approach my current role in the same way. I try very hard not to micromanage. Instead, it's my goal to make space for coaches and others to use their own talents and energy to create solid, successful teams. I try to do this by setting guidelines based on core values, such as integrity, trust, respect, teamwork and loyalty.

For example, respect is a core value of our program. To foster an atmosphere of respect in which everyone—both players and coaches—can achieve his or her best, we have general guidelines for how student athletes and staff will be treated within the program. We don't humiliate people. We don't denigrate them. We don't tear people down. It's my job to help coaches lead effectively within these guidelines, not to tell them to do a particular drill or run a certain play.

I want to be available to our staff, to help them in whatever ways I can. I am honored to work with a talented and dynamic group of leaders, and I feel privileged to mentor, even in a small way, the next great generation of coaches. The drills, plays and formations will change and evolve as time goes on, but focusing on values is always a winning strategy.

Coaching Coaches

While I have seen the positive effects of empowerment in government office and on the football field, I have also seen the damage that can be done when the opposite happens.

Prior to my return to Nebraska as athletic director, a consultant from the business world was hired to evaluate the athletic department. I think the idea was to improve performance, but things didn't seem to be working out well. Even though the consultant had been in the athletic department only 10 weeks, he was seeking to make some major changes. He was from the business world and had no specific knowledge of athletic departments. He required administrators to report to him rather than to the athletic director, reviewed emails that were sent out to make sure they were to his liking, and also had many closed-door meetings. As a result, a certain amount of mistrust had begun to pervade the athletic department.

This consultant was in the process of setting up a fairly elaborate system of evaluation and performance reviews, which would have taken a great deal of time to implement. The reviews would occur every 90 days, and cost of living raises would then be allocated based on those reviews. The only problem was that this particular plan would have been contrary to University policy. The situation had become somewhat dysfunctional, in that people were fearful for their jobs and no one felt very free to operate on their own initiative without first checking with the consultant. In the day or so that intervened between the previous athletic director's dismissal and my being hired, the staff fired the consultant, which was a fairly good indicator of how unpopular some of his reforms had been.

Part of my job, in my latest role, is to coach the athletic department staff. I want to see good effort and standout performance, but I also want to create an enjoyable place to work. Putting good people under the gun to ratchet up their level of accomplishment from one day to the next is, in my experience, not the best way to get the best out of them. Instead of creating a team-oriented environment that encourages collaboration and mutual trust, excessive focus on individual performance fosters unhealthy competition, division and dysfunction.

The damage done to the staff took a number of months to repair—such a high level of stress had stretched some almost to the breaking point, and unwinding the tension couldn't happen overnight. But my perception is that there is a growing sense of teamwork and support among departments and coaches, and people tell me they feel much better about going to work every day.

When those you lead feel cared for and valued as people, you will inevitably influence their attitude, self-esteem, and performance. This reminds me of something Trev Alberts, a linebacker from 1990-1993, had to say:

> Coach Osborne fostered an environment. He didn't allow negativism. He didn't allow assistant coaches who were constantly at our throats. They demanded an awful lot, but I was never cursed at. I was never told how worthless I was. Coach Osborne and his assistants didn't coach out of fear. Ultimately, when it comes down to it, third-and-one and you've got to get off the field, or fourth-and-one at the end of a game, who are you going to play for: the person you've developed a genuine respect and love for, someone who cares about you and your family, or someone who just screams and yells at you?

Erin Duncan, a young woman who worked for me in Congress as a Legislative Director, said the following:

> When I first joined Tom Osborne's staff, it was difficult to get used to his style in the office. We were essentially a group of strangers who suddenly had to work as a team. . . . We were a staff of young women—average age probably 25—not a bunch of football coaches desperate for

time with the Coach of the Century. For a
while it seemed like we spoke different languages, and we probably did. I can't really
pinpoint the tipping point for when the
staff gelled, but it just did, over time.

Tom was incredibly supportive of our
decisions as his staff and would trust our
judgment. There were many situations in
which we had to make decisions very
quickly. Staff was allowed to negotiate
with committees, for example . . . I always
appreciated how much trust he put in me
and how he always took my/our side on
an issue, regardless of the situation . . . He
trusted that we had done our homework
and had good intentions . . . it really gave
even very young staff a lot of responsibility and confidence . . . Perhaps the greatest lesson I learned from Tom was to let
others around you shine. The greatest testament to someone's leadership is how
supportive and encouraging he or she is
of others.

I do not mention this feedback to boost my
ego or to provide evidence that I have been an
effective leader. I'm sure that there are many
who have worked with me or for me who would
not have spoken so kindly about my leadership
style. However, these kind words remind me—
and speak as a testament to you—of the impact

a leader can have when they serve in a transformational way.

In my different roles in service, I wanted as much as possible to have the people who work for me and the players who played for me understand that we are all in this together. This is why during the last several years I coached at Nebraska I had the players themselves set goals for the whole team. Each one of them had written their particular objectives on a piece of paper of what they wanted to have happen. The staff and I collated them and picked the top priorities we would focus on that season. I believe that collaborative effort was much more effective than if they had no ownership in the process. I emphasized that the team goals were essentially their goals, so it was up to them to work with the coaches to achieve them.

It was amazing to see how many goals were achieved once we gave the players ownership. The last team I coached, in 1997, achieved every one of the seven goals they set.

UNITY

Transformational leaders have a particular mission in mind—whether to increase company growth, expand the resources of a non-profit organization, implement a new curriculum in a school, or prepare troops for battle. Whether you are currently leading others or preparing for future leadership, you will lead with a particular objective in mind. In order to complete your mission, there needs to be a cohesive and purposeful spirit among those who are following your lead. Partisanship needs to be eliminated and you must make a point of bringing about unity within your organization, staff, team or company. There will always be differences among people, but having a common purpose heals divisions.

On a Mission Together

At Nebraska, like most places, people like to win. They like to win football games, and they also like to win in all other sports. But our mission is not to win. The mission of the University of Nebraska athletics department is to "serve our student-athletes, coaches, staff and fans by displaying integrity in every decision and action; building and maintaining trust with others; giving respect to each person we encounter; pursuing unity of purpose through teamwork; and maintaining loyalty to student-athletes, coworkers, fans and the University of Nebraska."[1] It might be disconcerting for many fans to hear that our mission is not to win but rather to live out certain core values that, if properly followed, will lead to effective performance. But as John Wooden, the former UCLA basketball coach, pointed out, emphasizing the process rather than the final score is the key to maximizing performance.

When I came back to the athletic department in 2007, I could tell that something was not right. Some people were ready to quit. Some people had quit already. The first meeting I attended my first day on the job involved two mental health professionals who were offering ideas on stress management to members of the administrative staff. I could sense that there were serious stress and morale issues and that this was more than a casual exercise.

One of my first initiatives as the athletic director was to get everyone together—all 240 members of the department—to develop a mission statement. Just as I believe that a personal mission statement can be a powerful tool for making personal decisions according to one's values, so too I believe that a corporate or team mission statement can bring people together to achieve a common purpose.

I began by asking each person to name core values or principles that they felt were foundational to our department's success. Through a show of hands, we settled on the five core values of Nebraska's athletic program: integrity, trust, respect, teamwork and loyalty. These values would become the core of our mission. We wove these values into a mission statement that all the employees were encouraged to improve or alter through a series of emails. The final product was a group effort that came from the employees. It was not imposed from the top down.

Once we had a common purpose, a mission that nearly all wanted to fulfill, I met with each division in the athletics department to brainstorm ways that our common values and mission could be incorporated into their particular area of operation. How could the security people build and maintain trust? How could the food-service workers pursue unity of purpose through teamwork? How could the medical staff give respect to each person they encountered? How could each sport's coaching staff display integrity in every decision and action? How could my specific area, administration, maintain loyalty to student-athletes, coworkers, fans and the university?

I also did a lot of listening. It was important to me that each person in the department was given a chance to be heard, and that each person knew that he or she was valued. Out of that long process, I think that healing began to occur. It wasn't overnight, but gradually people became more trusting, felt more unified and showed more respect for each other.

9/11

There is quite a bit of disenchantment about "partisanship" in Washington. People ask, "Why can't Republicans and Democrats get along? Why is there so much bickering? Why can't they work together for the good of the whole country?" They can tell that much of the posturing and disagreeableness in evidence among Washington politicians is not for the sake of the country but in order to advance themselves or their party.

The sad truth is that the system is, for the most part, winner-takes-all. Whichever party is in the majority sets the legislative agenda and has all the committee chairs and a majority of members on each committee. All the minority party can do is act as "the opposition," doing its best to limit or modify the majority's initiatives in order to look better than those in power. The result is a highly partisan environment that seems to get worse as time goes on.

Having said that, I have seen firsthand how people with opposing ideologies can set aside their differences in times of crisis. The morning of 9/11, I was in my office in the Cannon Office Building when someone drew my attention to the TV, which showed images of the World Trade Center on fire. There was talk of a small plane that had perhaps flown off course and crashed into the building, but just then, the second plane flew straight for the other tower, and it became clear that what we were seeing was an attack, not an accident.

The alarm sounded, and we were evacuated from the building. My staff and I walked 20 minutes to my D.C. apartment because we wanted to stay together and we wanted to make sure our congressional leaders could reach us. As we walked, we could see smoke rising from the Pentagon while sirens screamed. The Pentagon had been hit and many lives had been lost. Al-Qaeda had attacked not only the symbol of our economic might but also that of our military power. We only found out later about Flight 93, which had crashed in Shanksville, Pennsylvania, but had apparently been meant for the Capitol building, which symbolizes our government.

My wife, Nancy, was in Washington at the time. Airports were closed, and people felt trapped. Nancy even looked into renting a car to drive to Nebraska, but I talked her out of it. Many people did leave by any available means of transportation.

That evening, we were all called to an emergency meeting. Speaker of the House Denny Hastert told us then that there were still 11 or 12 planes unaccounted for—those planes might or might not carry more terrorists intending to destroy themselves and everyone on board. We would be kept apprised of the situation, but now our country needed us to do our jobs with courage and cooperation. When the brief meeting concluded, members of both parties stood on the Capitol steps and together sang "God Bless America." It might seem melodramatic now, but at the time it was quite moving, and many of us had tears in our eyes.

There was a strong sense of unity and devotion to the country. The Department of Homeland Security was formed, airport security was tightened, the Patriot Act was passed, and communication between the State Department, FBI and Immigration was improved. All of this was done quickly and with a minimum of partisanship. Everyone was focused on the nation's welfare. I shall never forget that time and only wish the cohesiveness that formed among our nation's leaders lasted more than a few months.

Praying Together

Even in the rough-and-tumble atmosphere of party loyalties and personal ambition, there was one oasis of true bipartisanship in Washington:

the weekly congressional prayer breakfast. I looked forward each week to sharing a meal and a time of worship with my colleagues, both Republican and Democrat—it was one of the most uplifting hours in my schedule.

The speaker for each week's breakfast was a member of Congress. During my time there, we only made one exception: When Jordan's King Abdullah made a state visit, he specifically requested permission to address the congressional prayer breakfast. We were in a bit of a quandary because we had never made an exception before . . . but how do you say no to a king? In the end, we invited him to speak—and I'm glad we did. King Abdullah talked about the common heritage of Judaism, Christianity and Islam: All were born in the same area of the world and all consider Abraham, Isaac and Jacob their "founding fathers." Because of these common roots, he said, there are common values and ideas shared among all three; if we are to work for peace, we must focus on these commonalities rather than on our differences.

On all other days, however, the speaker was a congressman or congresswoman—and these folks were often very different from me, whether in terms of background, ideology or political positions. I admit that occasionally, when a colleague quite different from me got up to speak, I'd think, *I'm not so sure I want to hear what this person has to say*. But almost invariably, by the time he or she was finished speaking, I had gained a new appreciation for that person, as the general format was to share one's personal life story—often with a spiritual emphasis, but not always. People who run for Congress are somewhat unique. Anyone who is willing to open his or her life to that level of scrutiny and is willing to be subjected to the criticism and the exhausting schedule of a campaign is not ordinary. You may not like them or agree with them, but they are risk-takers and are interesting people.

One morning, Patrick Kennedy, a Democrat who represents the first district of Rhode Island, was the speaker. Patrick was raised in Massachusetts and is the son of Senator Ted Kennedy. Now, I don't have to tell you that Nebraska is a long way from Massachusetts—not just in miles but also in philosophy and outlook. And my rural, middle-class background is quite different than Patrick Kennedy's upbringing. When Patrick got up to speak, I had a few preconceived notions about him. But as he talked with great honesty and openness about where he came from and the things he had experienced in his life, I began to realize that those preconceptions were nowhere near the mark.

Yes, Patrick was raised in a world of privilege and opportunity, but his life has not been a bed of roses. His "fairy tale" family has been stricken again and again by untimely death and destructive substance abuse—and every Kennedy misfortune is trumpeted across the pages of the tabloids. He has had trouble with substance abuse, and much of his passion to care for Americans with mental illness springs from his own struggle with bipolar disorder.[2] As I listened to Patrick speak about what makes him tick, I empathized with this young man and all he had dealt with, and I respected how he was making an effort to channel what he had learned from his experiences into something good. As a result of that morning, the two of us got further acquainted and, I think, developed a healthy mutual respect. In fact, we ended up working together on a piece of legislation that worked to provide suicide prevention screening for young people across the country, the Garrett Lee Smith Act.

The opportunity for us, regardless of party, to set aside our agendas and come together for an hour every week meant a lot to me. It's interesting: not everyone in Congress is a Christian . . . not by a long shot. But I saw the same willingness to pray together there as I saw when people gathered from all over the world for the annual National Prayer Breakfast. The House and Senate weekly prayer breakfasts hosted the National Prayer Breakfast each February. (I was an honorary host in 2006.) Every year, approximately 2,000 people from many different religious and cultural backgrounds come together in Washington specifically to pray.

You might think that such an event would be divisive, but just the opposite is true. Many dinners and other events are held in conjunction with the prayer breakfast. It was interesting to see that people from many different faiths and cultures were interested in Jesus. They weren't interested in Christianity, but they did seem to be drawn to Jesus and His teachings. Most of us have a spiritual impulse that often transcends national, linguistic and sectarian bounds and binds us together. The National Prayer Breakfast is a powerful example of spiritual unity.

An Even Match

I was one of about a dozen people who met once a week with Speaker of the House Dennis Hastert. Denny and I related well because he had been an athlete and then a wrestling coach for many years, but I think he asked me to be a part of the group because I had a unique point of view: I was both a "freshman" congressman and someone who had been in an entirely different arena for a long period of time. I had a different life experience than most members of Congress, and I could see the happenings of Congress from a different perspective.

When we met each week, we talked, as you might expect, about legislation coming down the pike, but we also shared our insights into the mood of Congress—how well or poorly people were working together, who seemed to feel marginalized or upset. And then we might offer our advice to the Speaker about how to handle particularly thorny situations.

On one occasion, I felt bold enough to ask, "Denny, why don't we let the Democrats win one once in a while? Not every idea that originates with the Democrats is a threat to Republicans . . . and a few of them are pretty good! We should vote for legislation based on its merits, not on who initiated it." I was worried that many of my colleagues felt pressured by their party leadership to vote in a certain way to get an edge over the other party, rather than to enact good laws.

Denny responded by comparing the House of Representatives to an athletic contest in which the two teams are pretty evenly matched. Giving the other team a point could change the game, and the winning side (us) might never regain the advantage. I found this response surprising, because Denny was not, himself, a highly partisan person. He was very patient and a good listener, and I have great respect for him.

I'm sure that Denny's response was due at least in part to the fact that Tom Delay was the House Majority Leader at that time. Tom was a very powerful figure in that he was a prodigious fund-raiser and had helped a great many Republicans get elected to office. Tom also was highly partisan, and proud of it. He was opposed to the Democrats having any kind of victory, and because he was counting the votes, he let it be known that he was disappointed in Republicans who broke ranks. Many people have painted Tom in a negative light, and certainly some of this was deserved, but I also knew that Tom cared very deeply about young people and had been very active in promoting many charitable causes benefiting disadvantaged youngsters. He had a hard side and a soft side, and at times I saw both.

I would hear 20- and 30-year veterans talking about how terribly the Republicans were treated decades before by the Democrats. Some people had very long memories; they could recall, with startling detail, slights received 30 years ago at the hands of the other party. (I'm sure the Democrats had similarly long memories, but I usually only heard one side of the story!) All I could think, when I heard these recitations of past injuries, was that someone sometime must break the cycle of retribution and animosity. Nursing ancient grudges only stands in the way of working together. And when we cannot work together, we cannot serve the country's best interest. There are legitimate philosophical differences between Republicans and Democrats; however, the public has grown weary of political posturing and self-serving partisanship.

Notes

1. Nebraska Athletic Department Mission Statement at Huskers.com. http://www.huskers.com/SportSelect. dbml?DB_OEM_ID=100&KEY=&SPID=41&SP SID=3046 (accessed April 2009).

2. CNN Washington Bureau, "The Situation: Friday, May 5," CNN.com,. http://www.cnn.com/2006/POL ITICS/05/05/sr.fri/index.html; Stephen W. Smith, "Patrick Kennedy: I Wasn't Drinking," May 5, 2006, CBSNews.com.

5

MAKE A DIFFERENCE

When I retired from coaching, I did not envision a life of ease. The possibility of a second career in public service had been something I had occasionally thought about over the years. It wasn't attractive for its own sake—I didn't look forward to fund-raising or campaigning or the almost inevitable personal attacks that come with running for office. I had never enjoyed public scrutiny and media attention.

Still, I have always considered politics as important. If you're the chairman of a big bank or a multinational corporation, you might have incredible wealth and influence. But if you're elected to represent a group of Americans in the federal government, you have an opportunity to shape our country's future. This is not to say that influential leadership roles outside of politics do not exist, but only Congress can make major decisions affecting national defense, education and monetary policy.

Whether you are the leader of a community organization, a PR firm, a small group at your church, or the captain of your football team, leadership is important because it impacts the lives of others. Leadership will not result in beneficial outcomes unless you opt to take on the responsibility of making positive changes and creating an environment in which you influence others for the better. Becoming a leader for the sake of gaining a preeminent position or wielding power can be very destructive.

I saw a need—and opportunities to impact positive change—in Washington. Education, taxes, the military, our economy—these are some of the most pressing issues facing America in our time. And even though politics can be difficult, sometimes very negative and personal, we need people who will tackle these issues with our country's best interests at heart. Many well-qualified people won't run for office because of all the negatives, but someone has to do it. When I retired from coaching, I was concerned about the direction our country seemed to be taking. I felt that holding political office was one way to make a difference. That's why I ran for office.

Running for Office

I'd been out of coaching for about a year, still weighing my options. I had come to the conclusion that I had enough energy and drive to make a major push toward something, but I wanted to be confident about the direction I chose.

Some people knew that I was considering running for office in 2000, and many tried to get me to run for the Senate, as Bob Kerrey had recently decided not to run again. I considered the Senate, but it would mean six years in Washington, and I didn't know how my wife, Nancy, would hold up for six years or more away from our children and grandchildren. I didn't know how I would hold up, either—so I was more attracted to the House with its two-year terms. I planned to serve more than two years, but if it just wasn't working out, I could quit after one term.

About that time, Congressman Bill Barrett, who had represented Nebraska's Third District for five terms, decided to retire. The Third District geographically encompasses nearly 80 percent of the state and is much more rural than the other two districts. I had grown up there, as had my parents and grandparents, and I was concerned about the unique struggles facing that part of Nebraska. Many young people were moving to urban centers, away from the farms and small towns where they had grown up. This migration—perhaps a third of the population from 30 or 40 years ago—had made an impact not only on the financial situation of those communities, but it also had made the future uncertain for a particular way of life.

Even though I had roots in the Third District and attended college there, I had lived in Lincoln for 38 years, which was in the First District. Nancy and I did have a summer home in Ogallala, Nebraska, which is in the heart of the

Third District, and we spent a fair amount of time out there each year. Still, some viewed me as a "carpetbagger" in view of the fact that I was not a full-time resident. Actually, unknown to most people, in order to be elected to the House of Representatives, you do not have to live in the district that you are representing. The Constitution states that it is necessary only to be a citizen of the state that you are representing in the House of Representatives. I have recruited, hunted and fished so often all across the state, particularly in the western part, that I considered myself to be as much a citizen of the Third District as any other part of the state. Fortunately, most voters agreed with me.

Although I had no background in politics or civil service, I thought that I might be able, as the Third District's representative, to help. Not everyone thought as I did. Some had pigeonholed me as a coach and could imagine me as nothing but a coach. But I decided to run for Congress and was sure that my experiences outside of politics could contribute to being a good elected representative. If you are moving toward leadership, remember that it's not only experience in that particular position that will make you successful; it's often your outside experience and your commitment to serve others that will help make an impact.

Consider our country's founding fathers. These were men who were farmers, merchants and doctors, not professional politicians. When they were elected to office, they agreed to go to Washington (or Philadelphia, in the earliest days) for two, four, six or eight years. They left behind their professions to serve their country, but they planned in advance to return to their families and livelihoods. The civil service model then was much like military service is now.

In contrast, there are young people today who start their "political careers" while still in college. They work on a campaign or two while they're in school. After graduation, they go to work in a congressional office for a couple of years and then go to law school, planning their run for their state's legislature the year after they pass the bar exam. After that, it's just a matter of working their way up the political ladder, and before you know it, they have spent their entire lives doing nothing but politics.

Many of these people are smart, effective and well-intentioned. But I believe there is a great need in Washington, D.C., for people who are not professional politicians, who have spent a good number of years outside the political realm—people who will set aside their "real" careers for a time of civil service and then return home when that service is complete. I think that if we began to treat elected office in this way, there would be much less of what some have called "Potomac fever"; that attraction to power and importance that makes it difficult

to leave Washington. We would also benefit
from the real-world experiences that people of
different backgrounds and careers could bring
to bear on the most pressing issues of our day.
It was with these ideas in mind that I launched
my bid for Congress.

Representing the
Third District of Nebraska

I was elected to represent one of the largest
districts, land-wise, in the United States. Nebraska's Third District encompasses nearly
65,000 square miles and has a population just
shy of 600,000. People are spread out. The
Third District occupies nearly 80 percent of
the landmass of the state and is one of the
largest districts in the United States that is not
a single state.

Other sparsely populated states (such as
Montana, the Dakotas and Alaska) are very
large districts as well, which means that the
representatives for these districts travel. A lot.
The same was true for me. I spent three or four
days a week in Washington and then flew
home to Nebraska to meet with people in my
district. I visited every one of the Third District's 69 counties at least once a year—usually
more—and the miles added up quickly: 200,000
or so each and every year. I knew that in order
to suitably represent my constituents, I needed

to be present in the district. Sure, I had grown up in the Third District, but I did not presume that my experiences had taught me everything I needed to know.

Take, for instance, agriculture. You can't grow up in Nebraska without knowing a little bit about farming. Actually, I had spent four years in St. Paul, Nebraska, living with my grandparents during World War II. My granddad worked as a meat cutter in the local meat market during the day, but he also had several cows he milked every morning before delivering milk and butter to customers on his route. He had some pigs and chickens, and I can remember my grandmother occasionally beheading a chicken and cleaning it. So I knew a little bit about agriculture, but I was not steeped in farm policy the way I needed to be.

I also had to learn, very quickly, about education, health care, military issues, water policy and a host of other issues that impacted my district every day. To be honest, those early days of listening, learning and assimilating great amounts of information were stimulating. Gaining new knowledge has always been valuable and intellectually interesting for me, and I enjoyed the steep learning curve required. I didn't think I could effectively make a difference without doing my homework and knowing the details of my new job. A member of Congress needs to know something about a large number of topics, but it's impossible to be very knowledgeable in more than a few.

I think some people thought I would be tremendously frustrated with the slow pace of change in Washington, but I went with realistic expectations. I knew that getting things done wouldn't be quick or easy, and sometimes would be impossible. Yet, in fact, I was pleasantly surprised by what we were able to accomplish. I think three factors expedited things for me. First, I was fortunate enough to be a Republican at a time when Republicans were in the majority. That made it easier to get important legislation passed. Second, I had good relationships with Speaker of the House Denny Hastert and John Boehner, who was then Chair of Committee on Education and the Workforce (he is now the House Minority Leader). Those friendships gave me an opportunity to gain a hearing for my ideas that I otherwise might not have had. Third, I was not your typical freshman. I came to Congress with a coaching background that gave me an ability to get to know a great many members of Congress rather quickly. I was seen as something of an oddity and there was a curiosity factor, but after a few months the novelty wears off and people want to see how well you perform. You can have a great personality and be very charming, but the fact of the matter is that leadership is about execution—getting things done.

Equality and Democracy

As a culture, we have not always appreciated the contributions of women as equal to those of men. This is particularly true in the world of sports, but it reaches, I think, into every sector of society. This area was one of many that I purposefully sought to effect positive change.

My two daughters were involved in high school athletics. They did very well, and I've always appreciated that they had the opportunity to compete—you learn something in athletics that you can't learn anywhere else, and it's just as true for girls as it is for boys. My maternal grandmother was quite a good athlete, a golfer and a softball player, who still loved to talk about her years on the field when I was a boy and she was in her 60s. But in my mother's generation and then in mine, women were encouraged not to play sports. My wife, Nancy, has told me about girls' gym classes, which they called "body mechanics," in which they did gentle stretching but never anything rigorous or competitive. I think the mindset at the time was that women were too frail to compete—which is silly, as my grandmother could have told them.

Title IX, while it has been a mixed blessing in implementation, was an initiative for equality that was long overdue. I'm glad that women are being recognized, on the field and else-where, as strong and ready for the challenge, because their contributions to our culture are invaluable.

When I retired from coaching and went to Washington, I came from a nearly all-male environment to an office in which all but one staff member was female. The truth was that I had never worked much with women, and I had a lot to learn. I soon gained a great appreciation and respect for the female staffers in my office. They had superb organizational skills, excellent writing abilities and clarity of thought.

To be honest, until that experience, equality wasn't on my radar. It's not that I was sexist; I just hadn't had much opportunity or need to think much about it. I'm sure I still have a lot to learn, but now it is important to me—whether at the training table with Nebraska's female competitors, in the classroom with female students, or in the administrative office with female colleagues—to do what I can to help women and men be given an equal opportunity to succeed.

The Iraqi Women's Caucus

During my time in Congress, I tried to go to Iraq at least once a year. I wanted to meet with our troops and see for myself how the conflict was progressing, but I also was concerned about Iraqi civilians and how we might help them build their new democracy.

After a couple of trips, I was in a meeting with then-Deputy Secretary of Defense Paul Wolfowitz, Congresswoman Jennifer Dunn, and a few others. Paul was briefing a group of congressional representatives on national security and Middle East issues. As we talked, I expressed some of my concerns: "Obviously, there had been an awful lot of war in the Middle East for several generations and many young men have died. I wonder if it would be a good idea to focus some of our resources on women, who surely have a big part to play in Iraq's future." Both Paul and Jennifer were enthusiastic about the idea, so we began to brainstorm.

That initial conversation evolved with others' input and ideas and eventually became the Iraqi Women's Caucus. With some funding from the State Department, we invited women who were interested in being a part of Iraq's political process to come to Washington to learn about how democracy works. Previously, women had been shut out of Iraq's elections, but in their first constitution, the provisional Iraqi government mandated that at least a third of the parliament's seats would go to women. That meant that these ladies had some preparing to do.

Congressional representatives volunteered to meet periodically with groups of 10 to 12 Iraqi women to share what we knew about running for office, representing constituents, writing legislation and negotiating with other lawmakers.

But we also listened, and we were impacted by some of the horrific stories we heard. Every one of them had lost someone in Saddam Hussein's regime of terror, and many of them shared stories of children tortured in front of their parents or women raped in front of their husbands. It was unimaginable. They were grateful that they were now free of Saddam's regime.

One of the cultural differences we had to understand better was Sharia Law, which is the Islamic doctrine that governs many people's lives. Under Sharia, women are sometimes seen more as property than as people. They are not allowed to wear Western garb and must always keep their heads and faces covered. Most of them don't have the option to be active, politically or otherwise, outside the home.

In one of the first meetings of the Iraqi Women's Caucus in Washington, I was introduced to the group as one of the co-chairs of the meeting. I went around the room and began to shake hands with each woman. But one young lady jumped back and refused to shake my hand—she could not touch a man who was not her husband.

Sharia customs and practices were and still are very prevalent in Iraq. I remember meeting in the Green Zone in Baghdad with Ibrahim al-Jaafari, the prime minister. He had been educated in Britain and had, I think, been in the UK for the better part of 20 years. He could speak English just as well, if not better, than we could. But during our delegation's visit, PM al-Jaafari only spoke Arabic and waited for a translator to relay his words to us. He was very formal, very traditional and very Shi'ite. I discussed the Iraqi Women's Caucus with him and expressed our hope that he would include women in the political process going forward. I don't think I made much of an impression on him.

Whether Shi'ite, Sunni or Kurdish, many of the women who formed the Iraqi Women's Caucus were well educated. Some had gone to college or graduate school in the U.S., Europe or the Middle East. But not many had been given opportunities to use their gifts and intelligence in service to their communities. Now they had their chance.

We decided that it might be wise to have a meeting of the Iraqi Women's Caucus in the Middle East, so we chose a resort near the Dead Sea and several of us went to meet with them. As I recall, more than 300 women came to that conference from all over Iraq. Most of them had come by car, and many reported being shot at on the way from Iraq to Jordan. They took enormous personal risks to come, and it was likely that their presence at the conference increased the danger they would face when they returned home. (Later, in fact, several women whom I had gotten to know were assassinated during their campaigns for office.)

Altogether we made four trips to Iraq, one to Afghanistan and two or three to Kuwait. We often met with representatives from the Iraqi Women's Caucus. Sometimes we discussed the upcoming elections and campaigning and other political topics, but we branched out to other areas, too. We offered some financial support. We helped them set up a number of centers throughout Iraq where women could learn skills such as weaving, basic accounting and how to start a business. All of this was done to empower Iraq's women to take their places as partners in their country's future.

It all culminated, of course, in Iraq's first free elections. People stood in line for hours to vote, and dipped their thumbs in ink to show that they had participated in the election. There was massive turnout across the country, even under the threat of violence, and I couldn't help but admire the courage and sacrifice of those who had struggled to make it a reality.

In many parts of the world, the poor way women are treated stands in the way of economic, political, social and entrepreneurial success. I believe that one of the major reasons there is so much poverty and lack of progress in the Middle East is that the intelligence, energy and creativity that women bring to the table have been excluded. Involving women in the democratic process and in everyday life leads to a healthier and less violent society and a broader appreciation for the sanctity of human life. Women play a key role in strong democracies, and we ensure a brighter future when we offer them opportunities to excel.

The war in Iraq has been very controversial. Stockpiles of weapons of mass destruction were not found. We have lost many lives and have spent billions of dollars, yet as I talked to Iraqis and visited troops, I was convinced that the sacrifice may someday be seen as justified. A representative government in which people are valued and productive may serve as a beacon of what is possible to other countries in the region. Entrepreneurial activity has exploded, women have been given a voice and the dynamism associated with democracy has been unleashed. Other nations from that region may eventually follow suit. Just look at the boldness of those in neighboring Iran who protested the apparently fixed outcome of the 2009 presidential election there.

I say all of this to remind you, today's and tomorrow's leaders, that change is possible. Sometimes it takes a while to make a difference and certainly there will be obstacles along the way. The power of leadership lies not in the glamour of being in charge, but with the responsibility of taking the chance to influence the future in a positive way and to make the lives of others better.

A Difficult Leadership Assignment

On July 24, 1998, a gunman entered the east side of the United States Capitol and shot Detective John Gibson and Officer Jacob Chestnut, who were guarding the entrance to the Capitol. Both men died as a result of their injuries, and the gunman responsible was shot and captured. Both of the officers who had been killed had families with young children. A colleague of mine, Rick Renzi, decided that he would like to raise some money to provide scholarships for the children of the deceased officers and, because Rick was a former college football player at Northern Arizona, he thought that a benefit flag football game between members of Congress and the Capitol Police would be a good way to raise the money.

Because I was the only member of Congress who had a good deal of coaching experience, I was asked to coach the congressional team. I accepted the assignment with some misgivings, as I knew the Capitol Police had an organized flag football team that practiced regularly and played a set schedule of games. Also, they had a great many former college athletes on their team and were about 15 years younger on average than the congressional team that we would put together. For those readers unfamiliar with flag football, each player has a belt attached by Velcro with a flag or multiple flags attached to it. Rather than tackling the ball carrier, the defender strips the flag, which constitutes a "tackle." This doesn't sound very rough, but sometimes it is easier to knock the ball carrier to the ground and then grab the flag. No pads are worn, and blocking is fairly physical. In short, it can be a very rough game.

The first step in getting ready for the game was to get organized, so I scheduled three practices. It was difficult to get very many of the Congressmen together for practice. Even though we practiced early in the morning, we seldom had more than half of the squad together at one time. I would doubt that there was any member of the team who attended all three practices—most attended only two, and some were only in attendance for one practice.

The day we were to play the game arrived, and we went over to Gallaudet Stadium. Gallaudet, a school for the deaf located in Washington, D.C., did have a football field, but it was about as poorly a lit field as I can remember and it was raining. We were going to play in the mud, which was about three inches deep in most places on the field, so the task was truly a daunting one at that point. Somehow, our team performed better than I thought they had any chance of performing. We used some play action passes. Tim Ryan, a Congressman from the Youngstown, Ohio, area, played well at quarterback. He had played some college football at

Youngstown State, and even though he had a bad knee, exceeded my expectations.

I have several vivid recollections of the game. Kendrick Meeks, who had played college football and looked like one of our most talented players, ran a deep pass pattern during warm-ups and managed to pull both hamstrings and couldn't play. Bill Shuster had his ear torn mostly off in a pileup. Fortunately, he was able to get it sewed back on, but he was not able to finish the game. We had several bruises and other minor injuries. I remember turning around on the sideline and seeing Thad McCotter, one of the brightest people I have ever known in Congress, smoking a cigarette behind me on the sideline—something I had never witnessed in 36 years of coaching. Thad was playing defensive end and looked more like a college professor than a football player, but he played considerably above my expectations for him.

In short, it was a ragtag group; somewhat similar to the military unit that George Washington used when he crossed the Delaware to defeat the British. At the end of the game, the score was 14-14. I was amazed that we were able to pull off a tie and felt a little bit like Herb Brooks must have felt when his USA hockey team defeated the Russians in the Olympics many years ago.

We should have retired undefeated at that point; however, Rick Renzi organized another

game the next year, and things were even more
stacked against us. With memories of how rough
the game had been the year before, and with images of Bill Shuster's ear dangling, many of our
players decided they would no longer play flag
football against the Capitol Police, so we didn't
have very many players. In addition, the field in
game 2 was dry, which gave the much faster
Capitol Police even more of an advantage, and
the Capitol Police were bent on revenge. They
had been humiliated by the tie score the previous year and had redoubled their practices.
They were quite determined to make us look
as bad as possible.

The personalities of Congressmen show up
very clearly on the athletic field. We had a member—who shall go unnamed—who had some
speed and athleticism and was our free safety.
We played a three-deep zone pass defense, which
is about as simple as you can get in pass cover-
age, and I repeatedly informed the safety that
his only responsibility was to play the deep
third of the field and that he was to let no one
get behind him. Once the game started, he was
bent upon making a name for himself in the
game. He began to gamble by playing at linebacker depth and trying to intercept crossing
patterns instead of taking care of the deep third
of the field, which he had been assigned to cover.
As a result, we gave up four deep passes during
the game.

To make matters worse, our quarterback decided to ignore the plays that I sent in, which were drawn on pieces of cardboard. As he ad-libbed, we became more and more disorganized. Mary Bono, who ran for the seat vacated by the death of her husband, Sonny Bono, was carrying the plays to the huddle. Mary was the only female member of the team, and I thought that the best way to keep her healthy was to use her only as a messenger. I told Mary to tell the quarterback to run the play I called. I found out later that Mary had passed the message along using much saltier language than I had used. Then our quarterback got hurt, and we took a pretty sound whipping.

This was the last game that I coached, and it was a difficult way to wind up my coaching career. However, I did learn that coaching members of Congress is a little bit like herding cats. I had even more empathy for Denny Hastert, who had to move Congress forward as the Speaker of the House. On a brighter note, we did raise a fair amount of money for scholarships for the children of the slain policemen. I'm hoping that by now some of them are in college.

If a former coach is ever elected to Congress in the future, I would advise him not to coach a team comprised of members of Congress. The experience would prove to be unlike anything he had experienced before.

Not for the Faint of Heart

Becoming an effective leader means taking risks involved in making a difference. That is usually not easy and requires courage, strength of character, conviction, and a willingness to learn. Leadership involves perseverance, uncertainty and criticism. I found that especially to be true as it concerns running for public office.

When I first decided to run for governor, a politician friend said I should take a poll and use the results of that poll to formulate my platform. The idea was that I should find out what resonated with people and what didn't and then emphasize those points of view that had strong public approval while avoiding those issues that would result in losing votes. This approach did not square with my idea of leadership. It simply promotes the status quo; it has nothing to do with changing things for the better.

I told my friend, "No, I don't really need to take a poll to know what I'm all about. I'm going to tell people what I think needs to happen, what my vision is. If that doesn't resonate with them, then I'm not the guy they need." I lost the election, but I did feel good about the fact that I tried to communicate what seemed best and gave people a choice. I also felt good about the fact that the campaign was run in a positive manner. There were no negative ads and I certainly did not disparage my opponent. I can tell you, though, that winning is more enjoyable than losing.

I'm glad to have moved on to a new role, but I think often about my friends who still are serving in Congress. Most want to do the right thing for their states and for their country. Government is not perfect, and there are a few things we could do to make it run more smoothly and fairly. But I believe that many of the people who choose a life of public service are motivated by patriotism and a desire to do what's right. Those who are motivated by self-interest certainly tarnish the image of those who seek office for the right reasons.

Writing in the early 1800s, Alexis de Toqueville, a Frenchman, said, "America is great because America is good. If America ceases to be good, America will cease to be great." America is still good in many ways, but few can argue that our culture has not drifted badly in many other ways. Our "greatness" is certainly being challenged. Most Americans have less trust in government, business leaders, celebrities and even members of the clergy than they did a decade ago.

This erosion of trust in our leaders makes the democratic process more difficult, as democracy relies heavily on cooperation and trust. We are seeing a lack of effective leadership in government, athletics, business, education and even the Church. Without good leaders, we will have a difficult time maintaining a preeminent position among world powers.

6

DEALING WITH ADVERSITY

Adversity is a part of the human condition. No matter how effective your leadership is, you are going to encounter challenges and obstacles along your way. How you react to adversity will be the biggest thing that will determine your level of success.

Three Choices

When adversity strikes, I think we have three choices: The first is to quit. The second is to blame someone else. The third is to learn from the experience.

Abraham Lincoln is one of the most admired figures in history, and the success of his presidency is legendary even today. But some people don't know that long before he became president and fought to preserve the Union and end slavery, his life was stricken by one adversity after another. His family was impoverished when he was a child; they lost their homestead and had to live on public land. His mother died when he was nine. When he was a young man, his fiancée also passed away, and he went into a deep depression—he was bedridden with grief for the better part of two years. He could not afford to attend law school. He lost his first political campaign and many more after that.

It's hard for me to imagine what would have happened to our nation if Lincoln had thrown up his hands and quit in the face of so much hardship, or if he had spent his life blaming the many people who failed him instead of finding a way to succeed. He seems to have learned something from those early heartaches, and I believe they made him a better president. Rather than letting circumstances determine his course, Abraham Lincoln was proactive in moving toward what he wanted to accomplish. When he could not go to law school, he taught himself and was admitted to the Illinois state bar. Recalling his father's talent for telling stories, he practiced the arts of voice inflection and rhetoric until he gained a reputation as a formidable courtroom attorney and, later, a famous orator. He suffered many defeats in running for public office, yet he seemed to learn and grow with each defeat and eventually became, perhaps, our greatest president.

Losing and Winning Proactively

Athletic coaches face the same three choices: quit, blame or learn.

Losing occasionally is inevitable, even if your last loss was so long ago that you don't even remember it. I often remind Nebraska's current coaches and players of 1996. We had won 26 straight games and two national championships and, to tell you the truth, many players had started to doubt that we would ever lose again.

And then we went to Arizona State. The final score was 19-0. Arizona State had 19. We had the 0.

Coming back to Lincoln, you might have thought someone had died. All the talk was about how the dynasty was over, how my coaching was ineffective, and so on. It's ironic: One would think that after having won so many games in a row we might have been given a break, but just the opposite was true. The more we won, the more we were expected to win.

Any time you have a program that has been highly successful for a long period of time, people get used to winning. (They never get used to losing.) One of the difficult things about a successful program is that it's easy to be painted into a corner. If you won 10 games last season, then 10 wins this season is not good enough. And if you win 11 games, you're expected to go undefeated. And then, once you've had a couple of undefeated seasons, losing one game is a very big deal. Two losses make it a very bad year.

That kind of unrealistic expectation can make coaching and playing in a program with a long tradition of winning very stressful. And with that kind of stress, it's tempting to forget to see each and every game as an opportunity to learn something and then run with it. It was difficult to never really have an off-season, when no one is thinking or talking about football.

I think that's part of the stress our coaches and players have experienced during the past two years. Some people seemed to think that once we had a new coach, we'd break out of the gate with a 12-win season. It isn't that easy. Once a program slips, it takes time and effort to get it back on track.

It would have been easy, after our loss to Arizona State in '96, for the players and coaches to point fingers at each other or to give up on the possibility of having a great season. But we chose option 3. On Monday afternoon, we all got together and agreed that Saturday's stinging loss to Arizona State was the best thing that could happen to us. Now our weaknesses were exposed. Now we knew what we had to work on in order to be a great team.

We shifted our focus from the loss to what the loss could teach us. And what we learned resulted in nine straight wins and a trip to the Big 12 championship game. Unfortunately, we lost that game to Texas, but had we won it, we would have played for a national championship five straight years.

I sometimes talk to the current coaches at Nebraska about that year. I tell them that things are never as bad as they seem when they lose, and they are never as good as they seem when they win. The final score is only one measure of athletic success; even when we win, there are still things to learn. Every Monday morning is a new opportunity to ask, "What can we take away from Saturday's game that will make us better? Where do we go from here?" The key is to be proactive, whether we win or lose.

People who adopt a reactive stance toward adversity usually quit, give up easily or blame someone else for their failures. Seldom are they very effective. Those who see opportunity in difficulty and hardship, on the other hand, usually do much better in the long run.

The Power of Adversity

When I was a coach, I saw that adversity often brings a team together. That's exactly what happened in Washington in the days and months following 9/11. For three or four months after the attacks, there was tremendous cooperation in Washington. Both houses of Congress seemed to be permeated by an atmosphere of solidarity—a recognition that, in the end, we were all on the same team. As unpopular as the Patriot

Act has become among some people in recent
years, we realized that U.S. law enforcement
agencies must be given better tools to prevent
further attacks. Whether or not every facet of
that legislation should be kept on the books as
is, both parties came together very quickly to
do what was necessary during a time of national threat and enormous pressure.

Likewise, we were all determined to do whatever we could to facilitate greater cooperation
among the various law enforcement and intelligence agencies. One of the problems that became obvious quite early in our investigations
was a lack of communication between the FBI,
the CIA, U.S. immigration, the Justice Department and other bureaus, whether due to tech-
nology issues or turf battles. As the facts emerged,
it was clear that, had there been collaboration
between these agencies, the attacks of 9/11
might have been prevented while still in the
planning stages—but because each agency had
only fragments of information that it did not
share with the others, no one could put together
the pieces in time to prevent the tragic loss of
3,000 lives. Members of both parties saw the
need for more cooperation between these vital
agencies, and we passed legislation that included
the creation of the Department of Homeland
Security to make it happen.

We were all concerned about the safety of our
country, and this patriotic concern was much

greater than ideological differences or personal animosities. When we debated the legislation I just mentioned on the House floor, I saw no evidence of one-upmanship or attempts to humiliate the other party; instead, people offered their honest opinions about how best these laws might work. There were differences of opinion, as anyone would expect, but these differences were aired with a genuine desire to reach a compromise rather than to discredit the opposition.

Those four or five months were some of the most difficult and most rewarding of my life. I saw the good that a government by the people and of the people, when it focuses on being for the people, can do. Unfortunately, that time of cooperation did not last. That crisis prolonged a peace that could not be sustained. I suppose it was inevitable that, at some point, people would begin to think again of reelection—and campaigns mean business as usual when it comes to partisan politics.

The Pink Slip

Sometimes adversity shows up in the form of making unpleasant decisions. This is something that is demanded of me in my latest role. I never thought I'd ever have to fire a coach.

When Bill Callahan and his staff arrived in 2004, Turner Gill, the only holdover from Frank Solich's and my staff, asked me to talk to the new staff and explain those things pertaining to Nebraska football that were especially important and unique. I spent more than two hours reviewing the importance of walk-ons, how the Unity Council came to be and how it worked, the importance of goal setting, the philosophy behind our offense and defense, and our recruiting strategies and the uniqueness of our fan base. The staff listened politely, but I didn't think that much of anything I talked about gained much traction. I had the impression that previous NFL and college experience trumped anything that I had to offer.

I met with the football coaching staff again shortly after being named athletic director, and I told them that I would do anything I could do to support them. I was up front about the fact that we needed to win seven or eight games in the season at hand. If we could do that, then everything would be fine—we would rebuild the program from there. On the other hand, if the team only broke even or, worse, had another losing season, I would likely make some staffing changes. With that said, what could I do to help?

Some people have speculated that I was hired to fire Bill Callahan. This was not the case. I didn't know Bill well and had no animosity toward him. On the other hand, as I mentioned previously, I could sense that things weren't going well. I was sincere in wanting Bill and his staff to succeed. A coach hates to fire another coach.

We began to lose, and lose badly. As we went along, I met with the coaches every week or so to find out what they needed and to give input when I was asked. We lost the last game of the season to Colorado, which gave us a 5-7 record. The most disappointing thing about the season wasn't the seven losses, however, but the fact that as the season progressed, the players seemed to lose confidence and, at times, didn't play with intensity. This was distressing to those who cared about Nebraska football, as we had almost always been an excellent team as far as commitment and effort were concerned. Our team played hard in losing to Texas and played well in defeating Kansas State, but we weren't competitive in our games with USC, Missouri, Oklahoma State, Texas A&M, Kansas and Colorado, so the die was cast.

I met with head coach Bill Callahan the Monday morning following the Colorado game and told him that, under the circumstances, I would not renew his contract. I thought we needed to make a change. Then I sat down with each of the assistant coaches and told them that I would do whatever I could to help them find new jobs. There was a chance that the new head coach would ask some of them to stay, but it was not for me to decide. (In fact, two of them were asked to stay on after I hired Bo Pelini.)

When people read the sports pages and see that a coach is leaving, they often don't realize that many other people also lose their jobs: assistant coaches, sometimes administrative assistants, strength coaches, and others. When I resigned as head coach after the 1997 season, I made sure that the staff would remain for at least one year. This seldom happens in major college athletics, and I was fortunate to be in a position in which I could ensure the job security of those I was leaving behind. Likewise, when Bob Devaney stepped down in 1973, he made sure that everyone on his staff had a job. When I handed the job over to Frank Solich in 1998, there was a thread of continuity from Bob Devaney's hiring in 1962 until Frank's dismissal in 2003, 42 years during which Nebraska had the highest winning percentage in Division I football.

Next, I began a search for a new head football coach. After interviewing five coaches, the right choice became clear to me. Bo Pelini had been at Nebraska in 2003 as a defensive coordinator, and I had positive recommendations from both players and coaches who had worked with him then. From his time at Nebraska, at Oklahoma and then at Louisiana State, Bo had earned a reputation as a very good defensive coach—and that's where our team was most deficient.

I asked Chancellor Perlman if he would like to accompany me on a trip to Baton Rouge to interview Bo Pelini and then on to Atlanta, where a search firm would have four other head coaches for us to interview. We accomplished the interviews over a two-day period and talked to several men who had experienced considerable success as head coaches and had staffs of assistants already in place. Even though Bo Pelini wasn't a head coach, I chose him because I felt we needed to make a significant turnaround on defense. We had lost several games by large margins in the 2007 season, and we had a number of great offensive teams in the Big 12 that would be returning most of their starters and their quarterbacks in 2008. If we couldn't slow those people down, we would likely have another losing season, and then things would be in danger of unraveling badly.

Members of the media were quite interested in the hiring process, so they were tracking the tail number on the airplane we flew to Baton Rouge and Atlanta. It was reported that the plane had abruptly dropped several thousand feet—I don't remember this happening, but it did catch the attention of our families. Most coaches don't want their names mentioned in connection with a job search, so the interviews in Atlanta were very private. Any information as to who was interviewed did not come from Nebraska or the search firm we employed.

It was difficult not to hire Turner Gill, who was head coach at the University of Buffalo.

Turner had played for me and had coached for me for a number of years as an assistant. I was in his wedding. Turner had been at Buffalo for two years and had begun to turn that program around. However, I knew that Turner's main experience and expertise as a coach were on the offensive side of the ball, which was not an area where we needed the most help. I felt that Shawn Watson, the offensive coordinator under Bill Callahan, would be able to handle the offense well, so I had to look at who would do the best job of bringing the defense along and also be able to run the whole program effectively.

Telling Turner that I was not going to hire him was one of the hardest things I have had to do. I know that Turner wanted the job, understood the culture at Nebraska, and was someone who was a great person and a great role model. Turner staying at Buffalo, however, was great for that program, as he managed to win the Mid-American Conference and go to a bowl game. This was the first championship and the first bowl game for Buffalo in a generation. Turner has recently been hired as head football coach at the University of Kansas, and he will do an excellent job there.

I never imagined myself in a position to fire coaches—I had always been a coach, and I know firsthand how difficult a job coaching is. Letting Coach Callahan go was painful, but I felt that doing so was in the best long-term interest of Nebraska's football program. I tried to manage the transition as smoothly as possible, to minimize hurt feelings and bruised egos through a time of uncertainty and upheaval. I hope those involved saw it that way, too. When someone in leadership has to deliver bad news such as personnel changes, it is important to communicate clearly and often with those affected. I told the coaches what they needed to accomplish to keep their jobs, talked to them weekly about how I thought things were going, and then sat down with each of them personally when they were told they would not be retained. This was not easy to do. Sometimes people find out about losing their jobs from an email, a written notice or an intermediary sent by the boss. Sometimes players find out they are cut from a team by reading a roster on the locker room door. Even though people don't like to be let go, my experience has been that if communication is good, they at least feel that they have been treated with dignity and fairness.

If you are in a leadership position right now, chances are good that you have already found yourself in a position that required you to make some painful changes for the greater good. If you are a future leader, understand that you will surely face those times. Though these kinds of decisions are not easy to make, I've found that they are where personal growth happens. How you respond at a time when adversity strikes has a great bearing on yourself as well as those you lead and whether they will follow your example in learning from the struggle or allowing adversity to overwhelm them. Whatever action or attitude you exemplify is what those you lead will learn to emulate. This is why character development is essential for great leadership.

WHAT MATTERS MOST

I always felt that coaching was primarily teaching. You were not only teaching *X*s and *O*s but also teaching principles by which young people could deal with adversity, success, fame and fortune later on in their lives. If you are serving in a leadership role or want to do so in the future, focusing on character, principles and process rather than results will help you lead others to more meaningful and purposeful lives. This is how we can best serve those we lead.

On a Mission

I've been a long-time admirer and reader of Stephen R. Covey, founder of the Covey Leadership Center (now FranklinCovey®) and author of *The Seven Habits of Highly Effective People*. In this perennially bestselling book, Covey argues that to live a truly effective life, we must align ourselves with "true north" principles that will develop in us a strong character.

Character is very important to the book's premise. Covey writes about the process of researching the book and discovering that, in the literature written in the first 150 years of our nation's history, success is inseparable from strong character. A successful person was honest, generous, self-sacrificing and trustworthy. By contrast, in much of the literature written during the past 70 years, success is more about perception: influence, charisma, possessions and recognition. One of Covey's goals in writing *Seven Habits* was to reorient our concept of success toward character, rather than personality.

One of the true-north principles that can develop strong character is to begin with the end in mind. Many people wander their way through life, one appointment to the next, without thinking very deeply about their purpose or intentions. In response to this tendency, Covey recommends an interesting exercise: writing your own eulogy, including what you would want a family member, a business associate or a friend to say about you at your funeral. The focus of a eulogy is to remember and celebrate the character of the deceased, to highlight the kind of life he or she lived.

It's not difficult to see how such an exercise can help us dig down to the bedrock of what life is about. At my funeral, I'd like someone to say, in complete honesty, "Tom tried to serve. He was a person who did his best to live out his faith. He was not a phony. He did what he said he would do; he was consistent and his word was good." Whether or not someone will say it, I don't know. But I want to live in such a way that these comments are not too hard to imagine.

After writing the eulogy, Covey next recommends composing a personal mission statement that is consistent with the core values outlined in the eulogy. We can think of a personal mission statement like a personal Constitution, guiding the decisions we make to keep us on the right course, much as the U.S. Constitution guides our government to stay on the course set for us by the founding fathers. A mission statement can help us live with intention and purpose, prioritizing and focusing our attention, energy and passion on what is most important to us. As we drift off course, the mission statement keeps pulling us back to our core values and a life of purpose.

The process of writing a personal mission statement requires a good deal of reflection, because you are working backward from the things that you want someone to say about you to the kind of values and principles that you need to live by in order for those things to be true of your life. Articulating these core values is the heart of the matter; knowing and understanding your purpose—what gets you up in the morning and what brings you peace at night—is key to living an effective, fulfilled and truly successful life. It is easy to become distracted by busyness, money and promotions—things that in the final analysis aren't that important.

My personal mission statement is to serve and honor God in all things. Sounds pious, maybe a little too religious for some. However, as I stood on the sideline and watched a player fumble as we were about to put a game away, as an official's call turned a possible national championship into another loss, as I disciplined players and my own children, as I did my income taxes, what other mission statement could call me back to true north? What line in the sand could help me examine my actions in light of what God would have me do other than seeking what would honor Him? Living by this mission statement doesn't mean that I always got it right, but it does mean that I've always had a standard by which to measure everything I did—a standard that does not depend on my mood, on what others think or on what is expedient. With time and practice, imperfect as I am, I have gotten better at implementing the mission statement.

Think about your own life. Think of the leadership role you that are currently in. Think about the leadership role that you want to be in. More than thinking about what you seek to accomplish through this avenue, think about the kind of character that you want to display and the values and principles that you want to live by. Sound character, good values and core principles don't change. Circumstances, public opinion and emotions vary. If we are grounded in those things that don't change, we have a better chance to weave our way through life's obstacles intact.

Worldview and Character

Many years ago, I read Luke 9:24, and that verse has been instrumental in my spiritual walk ever since. It says, "Whoever wants to save his life will lose it, but whoever loses his life for me will save it." It made me think about all the ways I had been trying to save my life.

One of the primary ways that I had tried to save my life was through sports, mostly on account of my dad. Right after the attack on Pearl Harbor, my father joined the army to fight in World War II. He was old enough that he didn't have to go, but he was very patriotic. I was nearly five years old when he left, and I didn't see him again until I was almost 10.

I was proud of my dad when he came home, but I didn't really know him. He wasn't a real person to me; he was someone who wrote a letter once in a while, had fought in the Battle of the Bulge, and had sent my brother and me a German rifle, helmet, bayonet and even a military-style BB gun used to train the Hitler youth. But I wanted to know him, and it didn't take long for me to discover that sports was important to my dad and that maybe this was the way to get to know him and gain his approval. So I threw myself into football, baseball, basketball and track. If there were tryouts, I was there.

When I started playing sports, "saving my life" was the last thing on my mind. I just wanted my dad to be proud of me. But as the years passed, I gave more and more of my time, energy and devotion to excelling on the field, at the plate or under the basket. By the time I began to think about Jesus' words in the Gospel of Luke, sports had become my unconscious "sure bet" for salvation. If I played well and people approved of me, then I could feel good about myself—kind of neurotic, but that was pretty much how it was. Eventually, the second half of the verse began to make sense: If I wanted my life to be saved, I must lose it for Jesus' sake. I wasn't exactly sure what this might mean, but I figured it began with trying to put Him ahead of everything else in my life—including sports.

I haven't always succeeded. It has been too easy to let other things consume me. Even after I was done playing pro ball, I threw myself into my graduate studies, first earning a master's degree and then a Ph.D. In hindsight, my studies consumed me far more than they should have. Then I became an assistant football coach. I decided that becoming a head coach would make my life more significant and secure. I even set a deadline: age 35. I thought that if I wasn't a head coach by age 35, I would be too old, so I would go back to an academic life. You might say that I was going to try to save my life by becoming a head coach.

Bob Devaney decided to step down as head coach after the 1972 season. In his last four seasons, his teams had gone 9-2, 12-0-1, 13-0 and

9-2-1 and had won two national championships, so the bar was set very, very high. I knew that we would have to win a lot of games to stay employed. That pressure to win, at times, made winning football games another way I tried to save my life. Then I ran for public office, and winning elections fought for the top spot on my priority list.

Keeping my priorities in order has been a life-long struggle for me. But along the way, my public decisions and personal choices have been deeply influenced by a particular view of the world. I believe that a person's character is greatly influenced by his or her understanding of how things are connected. I know that in my own situation, my faith—the way I view creation and the order of things—has had a major impact on how I see everything else.

As I survey the cultural landscape in the West, and particularly here in the United States, I see a clash between secularism and Christianity. I think that we are seeing a tug-of-war between these competing worldviews. On one side, there are people who see a clear difference between right and wrong. They believe that in order for a society to function fairly and justly, the difference between good and evil must be acknowledged. On the other side, there are people who see right and wrong as personal preferences that should be left up to an individual's personal feelings. However, in drawing this distinction, it is important to point out that a rigid, judgmental, condemning form of Christianity can be very hurtful and very "un-Christian." Unfortunately, this type of Christianity is what many people think of when they consider the Christian faith, much as many think of Islamic extremism when they examine Islam.

I think we see the effects of this tug-of-war at work not only in today's athletes, coaches and sports programs, but in the political landscape as well. Instead of focusing on what is right, too many leaders focus on gaining popular opinion or approval. It doesn't end there. Some of the greatest contributors to our economic difficulties have been unethical and illegal practices by decision makers in our business community. These people have been so focused on short-term financial gain at any cost that there has been a worldwide ripple effect that has been devastating.

This is why worldview is so important as it concerns our character. A person's view of the world tells a lot about what kind of person he will be on and off the field or in and out of the conference room, the trading floor, or the political seat. If he trusts a moral authority that transcends his own feelings, he will usually make decisions based on that worldview and live his life according to those higher principles. But if he trusts in his feelings as the final moral authority, he often will not lead a life of integrity and will make decisions only on the basis of furthering his own self-interest. The same is true in business, politics and family life.

It's Not About the Bottom Line

It is not always obvious at first glance how to best serve others, and trying to make those moment-by-moment decisions can be difficult. My early-morning routine has long been helpful to me in this regard.

When I was coaching, I woke up at 5:30 a.m. each day to spend 45 minutes or so in prayer and meditation. After getting ready for the day, I arrived at work by 7:00, where I gathered with the rest of the coaching staff for a short time of devotion. One of the coaches would read a verse of Scripture, talk about how that passage had impacted his life and suggest ways that it might affect our team, and then we closed in prayer. The devotional time usually only lasted about 10 minutes or so and was not a requirement for anyone on staff, but nearly everyone attended each and every day. It didn't seem to matter whether or not every person was a believer—the time of spiritual focus, regardless of each person's beliefs, seemed to get everyone off on the right foot.

Another thing that has been helpful is the example of John Wooden. Early in my coaching career, I read one of Coach Wooden's books, in which he quoted Cervantes: "The journey is better than the inn." For Coach Wooden, this meant that the process took precedence over the end result—and he lived and coached with this in mind. He started each new season by showing his UCLA basketball players how to properly put on their socks to avoid getting blisters. He focused on the fundamentals of dribbling, passing and shooting, and his practices emphasized running drills with speed and intensity. His definition of "success" was "peace of mind which is a direct result of self-satisfaction in knowing you did your best to become the best that you are capable of becoming."[1] Wooden believed that if his players were diligent in preparing to play their very best, the final score would take care of itself.

John Wooden had a powerful influence on my life. Shortly before his death, my wife, Nancy, and I visited him at his home in Los Angeles. He was still very sharp and was kind and gracious. His focus on the process rather than the final score, his never mentioning the word "winning" to his players, spoke volumes to me as a young coach. I began to worry less about outcomes and focused more on diligent preparation, an adherence to principle rather than the opinion of others, and relationships rather than material rewards. Shifting my focus early in my career to the process, the journey, rather than the final score, was very freeing. I cannot control the end results; they are largely out of my hands. I can, however, work hard and serve the best way I know how—and the peace of mind that comes with preparation and diligent service is success enough.

Our culture is increasingly obsessed with the bottom line, with the final score. The great temptation when results are the focus, unfortunately, is to cut corners. We see this in business, in politics, in sports and in relationships—ethics, principles, values and character are the first things to go when the bottom line is the only line that matters. In athletics, the mindset of "if we can't beat them, we had better join them" was often the response to schools that were cheating. In the corporate world, the pressure to beat earnings estimates and increase the stock price every 90 days often results in short-term unethical behavior. Enron reported projected future earnings as actual current earnings; this practice boosted the stock price but eventually led to an implosion of the company.

When we focus on the journey, on the other hand, we realize that the way we do things matters more than the profit margin, the vote tally, the scoreboard or who "won" the fight about the kids. And when we do things the right way— with honesty, integrity, generosity and respect for others—we experience the peace of mind that is the true indication of success.

There was a person in the athletic department here at Nebraska many years ago who was a nice man and did his job well. But it seems like every time I spoke with him, he couldn't stop talking about his retirement. He was doing his job, which he was good at but didn't enjoy very much, to pay for his retirement—and it was going to be great! He had plans for everything he was going to do after he retired, all the places he would visit. He was living his life for retirement.

After this man retired, his health went downhill extremely fast and he never got to do all the things he had planned. It was very sad, not just because he died somewhat prematurely, but because he had lived his entire life as a prelude to a retirement "paradise" that never materialized.

Like many football fans around the country, I have been watching Bobby Bowden and Joe Paterno continue to coach into their eighties. Both of these men coached for an exceptionally long time (Bobby has just retired). Knowing both of them as I do, my guess is that they coached so long because they enjoy it. They like the challenge, and they appreciate the association they have with their players. Both of them have good coordinators to handle the Xs and Os, are good recruiters, and are excellent leaders and managers of their teams. I suspect that the journey is the most important thing for them and that they have a hard time envisioning themselves doing anything other than coaching.

I remember Bear Bryant as he neared the age of 70, which at the time was about as long as any major college coach had ever coached the game, saying that when he quit coaching, he would probably "croak." It wasn't long before he did leave coaching, just past his seventieth birthday, and within a few months he indeed did pass away. The official cause of his death was a massive heart attack; however, I would imagine that the stresses involved in leaving something he did so well for a long period of time and that he enjoyed very much may have been a major contributor to his fatal heart attack.

That brings me to my current situation. As many Nebraska fans know, I was named the Interim Athletic Director in October 2007. I was given that title so that I could provide some stability to the athletic department for an undetermined, but relatively brief, period of time. Not long after taking the job, I talked to Chancellor Perlman about my concerns that the term "interim" made it somewhat difficult for me to make the moves I felt were necessary for the long-term stability of the athletic department. He removed the title, and I was given a date-certain when I would leave the position after the search had occurred for a new athletic director. The time specified was June 2010.

More recently, the chancellor and I visited and I told him that I had no problem with leaving in June 2010, or earlier for that matter, but that having a departure date etched in stone would result in a great deal of speculation on the part of fans and media as to who was next in line, who should be interviewed and what direction the department should take under the new athletic director. I felt that this would be a distraction for players, coaches and fans and would not serve the program well. As a result, we took the date-certain out of the equation, and I will stay for an unspecified period of time. The chancellor and I will each evaluate the situation annually. If at any time he feels that it is time for me to go, I will step aside, or if I feel that I can no longer serve the athletic department as well as a new person could, I will leave.

I enjoy what I am doing, but I'm certainly not in it for money or ego gratification. Also, there are some things that Nancy and I want to do before we kick the bucket. At the present time, I feel that I can make a contribution to the football program. I can help our programs in recruiting and can offer some sense of stability and permanence. I am also quite interested in making sure that our men's and women's teams have adequate facilities, which will help them to be competitive on a national basis.

We have a number of sports that are functioning quite well and could do as well without me as with me. So, there will come a time when I will leave. That day holds no special concern for me, as I know my fundamental mission— serving others in a way that can be consistent with my faith—can be accomplished in other settings. I want to be faithful to that mission right until the end.

We do not know when our lives will come to a close. It might be years from now after a long illness that gives us a chance to tie up loose ends and to let everyone important in our lives know how much they are loved. Or it might be sooner than we think. Remember Brook Berringer. We can't control the end results, but we can invest in service to others and in relationships while we're here. This is how we create a legacy that has a ripple effect through many future generations. As we influence a person, that person influences another, and the torch is passed on and on to others. Hopefully, the world is a better place for our having been here.

Note

1. John Wooden and Jay Carty, *Coach Wooden's Pyramid of Success* (Ventura, CA: Regal, 2005), p. 17.

LEAVING A LEGACY

It seems to me that some people are very conscious about leaving a legacy. You sometimes hear about a president's concern over how history will remember him, and about his efforts to get things done the last year or two he is in office in order to make his mark in a particular way. Or you hear about an actor who wants to be seen as creative or expressive or shocking, and chooses to work on a film based on how it might affect how he or she is remembered. For a politician, his or her legislative initiatives, peace accords and economic proposals all play a part in the quest for a legacy. I guess for authors, it's the number of books sold or the number of times on the bestseller lists. In the same way, coaches concerned with legacy often focus on their win-loss records.

I never thought too much about leaving a legacy as it related to wins and losses. I remember talking years ago to Ron Brown, one of our coaches at Nebraska and host of *Sharing the Victory*, the national radio show produced by the Fellowship of Christian Athletes. Ron told me, "Your legacy is not going to be about championships and wins and losses. It's going to be about things that have to do with the development of players—spiritual matters—how players are treated, whether they grow personally or not."

I believe Ron spoke the truth. I've had many former players, who are now successful in a variety of professions, say, "You know, some of the most important years of my life were the years I spent as a football player at Nebraska learning about perseverance and discipline and character." If there is any legacy, that is it. It isn't how many games or championships we won, even though we all cherish those milestones. Those former players influence their children, the kids they coach and the people they work with on a daily basis. If their years in the Cornhusker football program equipped them to pass on the values they learned here, that's all the legacy I could ever ask for.

The Legacy of Mentorship

One of the best ways to leave a legacy is to be a mentor. I see mentoring the next generation as an important part of the coming renewal. I believe that being a mentor is not only an investment in the life of one child but also an investment in the future of our nation. Effective mentoring doesn't happen by accident; it takes a sustained, concerted effort to form a relationship characterized by unconditional love and acceptance.

If you are a leader or strive to be one, one of the biggest contributions you can make in your community—and in the long run, our society as a whole—is by mentoring. When you make an investment in one person's life in this way, it pays dividends in the lives of many. I believe that a mentor makes three basic contributions to the life of a young person.

Vision is the first contribution a mentor can make to a mentee's life. So many young people grow up in a situation where they lack a vision for what is possible in their lives. They may have never seen a person in their immediate family graduate from college (or sometimes even high school). They may have grown up without a father. Their knowledge about how to apply for college or technical school may be very limited. A mentor can help them imagine a successful future and can guide them through the process of making the right choices along the way.

Second, a mentor shows his or her mentee unconditional care. In its original language, the Bible calls this kind of sacrificial love *agape*, which is positive regard without conditions. It's not a warm fuzzy feeling but an unwavering commitment to another person. This is particularly important when we consider how difficult relationships with teenagers can be. Mentors don't always feel warmth and affection for their mentees during the adolescent years. Nevertheless, good mentors choose to treat their mentees with respect and care, and this kind of consistent love from an adult can be extraordinarily powerful in the life of a young person. We can will the best possible outcome for their lives irrespective of our emotions. Many teens find the effect of unconditional love to be transformational.

The third contribution a mentor can make to the life of a young person is affirmation. Many youth do not receive much positive feedback, and it is difficult to achieve when they do not feel valued. Having someone who believes that they can accomplish great things is a powerful catalyst for achievement. In coaching, I saw how powerful affirmation is. The words "I believe in you," "I know you can do it" and "You will play a great game today" were very important. Many times, players achieved things they did not know they were capable of.

Servant-Leader Mentor

I'll be honest: I am often busy. Being the athletic director at the University of Nebraska means that I go to a lot of meetings. If I'm not in a meeting, I'm on my way to a meeting or on a conference call instead of a meeting.

As busy as this job keeps me, however, there is one appointment that I keep each and every week: the hour that I spend with the young man to whom I am a mentor. My assistant schedules a noon hour once a week when I bring my lunch and eat with him. We talk about school or football (he plays in the youth league) or sometimes fishing. Occasionally, if he's having trouble with his homework, I help him out or talk with his teachers about how he is doing. We try to focus on those things he does well—his strengths.

My time with him is something I never miss because showing up, each and every time, is the most fundamental aspect of being a mentor. When I recruit new mentors for TeamMates, the mentoring program I started with my wife in 1991, this is the message I try to communicate: Unless you come to mentoring with the mindset of a servant—a deliberate determination to put your mentee's needs ahead of your own for at least an hour a week—you won't be very good at it. Mentoring is serving.

There is another young man whose life I've been involved in recently who lost his dad, who played football for Nebraska. His father's death had taken a terrible toll on this young man, and his schoolwork was beginning to suffer. He had been in and out of foster homes and his teachers were concerned about him. The young man's mentor was able to understand that much of what he needed was help in processing his grief, rather than tutoring or intensive help with his education. We dug up film of his dad playing at Nebraska and gave it to him on DVD, reminding him that if he wanted to follow in his father's footsteps to college, he'd have to knuckle down in his studies. He was proud and pleased as he watched films of his father's football career. His teacher asked him to show the DVD to his class, which he did with great pride. Before long, his grades began to improve. The connection with his father, in the form of that DVD, helped the young man get things back on track. His mentor has been the one constant anchor in his life.

You can live each day with your legacy in mind. You can make a difference in the lives around you—whether those who are under your direct leadership, or those even in your family, church or community. When you strive to be a great leader, it's all about the journey and the positive changes you have effected in the lives of those who needed to be guided, mentored, or given a glimmer of hope into the future.

With the End in Mind

I think again of Covey's commission to "begin with the end in mind." Many folks believe leadership is measured in terms of success. So what is success? Is it just about winning? Acclaim? Trophies? Wealth? Our personal happiness or satisfaction? I have been blessed to experience some of these over the years, and I can answer without batting an eye: No. Accomplishments, applause, awards and fortune are rewards that

often come as a result of hard work and a determined spirit, but there is something bigger.
Something better. Something that will outlast
the winning season, the plushest corner office,
the heftiest bonus and the loudest cheers. That
something can only be found when we look beyond the final score.

Bob Devaney, the head coach of the Nebraska
Cornhuskers football team from 1962 to 1972,
and the man who helped to launch my coaching career, understood this well. When I last
went to see him, I knew that Bob was dying. His
family had made the difficult decision to re-
move him from life support, and I wanted to
see him while he was still lucid enough to know
that I was there.

As I sat by the bedside of this larger-than-life
friend who had been a presence in my life and
career for so many years, I couldn't help but reflect on the nature of success. Bob's wife and
his children had gathered around to share with
him and each other whatever time he had left.
He'd had a stroke, which made it very difficult
for him to speak, but he wouldn't let a little
thing like a stroke stop him. He knew he didn't
have much time left, and he wanted to make
sure the people who were most important to
him knew that he loved them.

When he could get a few words out, Bob didn't
talk about being named NCAA Coach of the
Year in 1971. He didn't talk about the national

championships Nebraska had won during his tenure as football coach. He didn't mention the money he had made over the decades of his successful career. What mattered to Bob at the end were his family and friends—the relationships that made him who he was.

Even though Bob was not known to be a religious man, he nodded his head when I asked if I could say a prayer for him. A tear rolled down his cheek as I finished, and I knew that the prayer had been significant to him. At the end, relationships, family and spiritual matters are often the only things that count.

I've had the privilege to have been with a number of people at or near the end of their lives, and something I've never heard even one of them say is "I wish I'd spent less time with my family" or "I really should have focused on making more money" or "If only I had worked longer hours!" Sadly, I have heard people near the end of their lives express a wish to go back and do things differently, to focus on what is actually important rather than chasing after things that cannot last.

In your present leadership role or the one in which you will find yourself in the future, remember it's not about numbers, how powerful you are, the number of championship titles you earned, or how well-liked you are; it's about how you lived your life and how you influenced the lives of others. I believe that is the true secret to great leadership.

Whatever legacy I leave is written on the hearts of the players I coached, through the way we treated them and in the values we promoted. I hope it is also written on some of the hearts of the people with whom I served on Capitol Hill, the people in my congressional district and the people who now work with me in Nebraska's athletic department. And I pray it will be written on the hearts of the children who are a part of the TeamMates mentoring program. There is no way to calculate a win-loss record when it comes to them. There is only a determination to make a difference, one child at a time.

What will you leave behind? How will others remember you? What is your legacy? Don't take leadership opportunities for granted. You only pass this way once, so make every opportunity to serve count.

THANKS

To write a book takes a team. I could not have done this without the help of many others who contributed their expertise, time and hard work. I want to say thank you to:

My wife, Nancy, who stood with me as we lived out the moments recorded in this book, sacrificed much and gave of her time to help review the manuscript, even during one of my fishing trips!

To Erin Duncan, my son, Michael, and my daughters Suzanne and Ann for diligently reviewing this book to make sure all the facts were recorded correctly.

To my assistants, Anne Hackbart and Sandy McLaughlin, who exemplify an attitude of excellence and putting others first.

To Jonathan Clements, who dreamed up this project.

To the team at Regal Books who have carried out this vision, particularly Regal president Bill Greig III, cover designer Rob Williams, managing editor Mark Weising, and editors Vanessa Chandler, Amy Gregory, Aly Hawkins, Steven Lawson and Alanna Swanson.

TEAMMATES

A portion of the proceeds from this book will go to TeamMates to help equip a new generation of leaders and to the University of Nebraska Athletics Student Life Center. If you would like to donate money to either organization, or to learn more information, contact:

TeamMates Mentoring Program
6801 O Street
Lincoln, Nebraska 68510
www.teammates.org

Nebraska Athletics Development Office
One Memorial Stadium
Lincoln, Nebraska 68588-0154
www.huskers.com

To find out more about booking Tom Osborne at your next event, contact:

Jonathan Clements
Wheelhouse Literary Group
P.O. Box 110909
Nashville, Tennessee 37222
info@wheelhouseliterarygroup.com

To obtain Nebraska football and Tom Osborne videos and memorabilia, log on to:

www.bestofbigred.com

ALSO BY
TOM OSBORNE

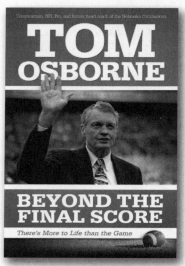

ISBN-13: 978-0-8307-5111-2
ISBN-10: 0-8307-5111-4

In *Beyond the Final Score,* Coach Tom Osborne chronicles his years as a congressman, educator, family man, mentor and now athletic director and reveals the character, values and faith that have grounded him throughout his incredible journey. This is a rare book in which an American legend brings wisdom, sensibility, dignity and spirituality to culture, worldview, politics, leadership and what really matters in everyday life.

Regal
God's Word for Your World™

www.regalbooks.com